CW00727616

After obtaining a first in English and Related Literature at the University of York, followed by an MA in Modern and Post-modern Poetry, Rob Warner joined Hodder and Stoughton as an editor in the Christian Books division. He rose in two years to be the publisher responsible for the division. Rob subsequently trained for the Baptist ministry, securing a first in Theology from the University of Oxford. He is joint chair of Mainstream, the Baptist Word and Spirit Network and a member of the Council of the Evangelical Alliance with whom he has worked closely on several projects, notably the Younger Leaders' Initiative and the 1996 Assembly of Evangelicals.

Rob has emerged in recent years as a prominent Bible teacher and a widely respected Christian writer, on themes including the person and work of the Holy Spirit, prayer and spirituality, building a mission-centred church, revival, social ethics, and the future of evangelicalism. His recent book, *The Ten Commandments and the Decline of the West*, was distributed by Spring Harvest to every British Member of Parliament. He travels widely from Queen's Road Church, Wimbledon, speaking at many national conferences, regional celebrations and leadership training days. In 1998 he has launched two weekly programmes on Premier Radio, one exploring leadership issues and one broadcasting his preaching. He has been married to Claire for nearly twenty years. They have two teenage sons, James and Tom, and a demented Labrador.

By the same author:
The Ten Commandments and the Decline of the West

The Sermon on the Mount

ROB WARNER

KINGSWAY PUBLICATIONS
EASTBOURNE

Copyright © Rob Warner 1998

The right of Rob Warner to be identified as
author of this work has been asserted by him in
accordance with the Copyright, Designs
and Patents Act 1988.

First published 1998

All rights reserved.
No part of this publication may be reproduced or
transmitted in any form or by any means, electronic
or mechanical, including photocopy, recording, or any
information storage and retrieval systems, without
permission in writing from the publisher.

Unless otherwise indicated, biblical quotations are from
the New International Version © 1973, 1978, 1984
by the International Bible Society.

Co-published in South Africa with
SCB Publishers
Cornelis Struik House, 80 McKenzie Street
Cape Town 8001, South Africa.
Reg no 04/02203/06

ISBN 0 85476 755 X

Designed and produced by Bookprint Creative Services
P.O. Box 827, BN21 3YJ, England, for
KINGSWAY PUBLICATIONS
Lottbridge Drove, Eastbourne, East Sussex BN23 6NT.
Printed in Great Britain.

Contents

for George and Doreen

Introduction

D. H. Lawrence once observed that the followers of Jesus would have to look a lot more like their Master if his teaching was going to be taken seriously in the modern world. The charge is not altogether unfair. Although the Christian witness always and rightly points to the excellence of Jesus, the supreme moral insights and authority of his teaching, the pre-eminence of his conduct in life and in death, there needs to be at least some consonance between the Saviour's teaching and his followers' way of life.

Sociologists speak about a plausibility structure. In the pluralistic smorgasbord of the late twentieth century, huge numbers of different religious and ethical perspectives compete for attention. It would be quite impossible to give every conceivable perspective a full and fair hearing, a rigorous examination. This means that a preliminary question is habitually asked. In order to determine whether a religion is worth the effort of careful examination – 'Does it make sense?' – people must first make a judgement about its followers: 'Do their beliefs improve their lives?'

As we approach the end of the twentieth century, the Western world is characterised by three trends. *First, there is a growing sense of spiritual vacuum.* Secular materialism attempted to sweep away religion as mere superstition. Consumerism suggested that our every need could be met in the shopping mall. But now we are faced by a revolt of the human spirit against such constrictions. Western society is becoming more religious once again, as people recognise that spirituality is an integral part of the human condition. Our world has embarked upon a new spiritual quest.

Second, there is a growing sense of moral bankruptcy. T. S. Eliot described our society as the first to attempt to live without reference to any god. By the late sixties, moral absolutes were being consigned to the ash heap of history. Western civilisation had been built upon the Judaeo–Christian ethic, which made a direct connection between ethics and God, who was seen as the source of moral absolutes. Without God, morality was increasingly dependent upon the consensus of public opinion. In just a few years we were left with only one moral absolute: it became compulsory to be tolerant of the immorality of others. We entered a brave new world of do-it-yourself ethics, in which everyone was entitled to do what was right in their own eyes. By the mid nineties our society was facing unprecedented levels of marital breakdown, urban ghettoes of lawlessness, a callous disregard for the poor and weak and elderly, the collapse in many towns and cities of any sense of local community or neighbourliness, and a growing disrespect for all authority figures from teachers to the police. Politicians and journalists have begun to agonise in public about the amoral anarchy that has overtaken Western society. Former champions of libertarianism have begun to become apprehensive of the disastrous consequences for our civilisation once children are no longer able or willing to discriminate between right and wrong.

Third, the vast majority of the population has not turned to the church for answers. For many, the church is part of the problem, not part of the solution. The new spiritual quest is far more likely to embrace Westernised hybrids of Hinduism and Buddhism. Eastern mysticism seems more attractive to the post-modern world than classical Christianity. The common assumption is that the church has been found wanting, that Christianity has been given its chance among us and it simply has not worked. We have become a museum piece, a part of Western heritage that no longer connects with present-day life and is generally considered unlikely to have any future relevance.

The new quickening of spiritual and moral debate has created opportunities for the Christian gospel unprecedented in the West for more than a century. But our proclamation is doomed to be ignored if our lives lack credibility. When the church fails to demonstrate the gospel as lifestyle the witness of our words will fall on deaf ears. This gives no Christian believer any excuse to denounce the church. As Karl Barth observed, we are called to love the church because Christ loves the church. Furthermore, we must always set the urgent need for credible discipleship as a yardstick against our own lives, for every professing disciple has contributed in some measure to the present weakness of the church.

The modern church is not short of strategies for advance, and we should be grateful for the many invaluable insights that can be drawn from movements working for biblical reform, spiritual renewal, cultural relevance, mobilisation in mission, church growth and so on. Nonetheless, the credibility of the church depends above all not on what we seek to do for Christ, but on who we are in Christ. Being is more fundamental than doing, character is more compelling than frenetic action, relationships come before strategic initiatives. When Jesus was asked to summarise the Law, he unhesitatingly quoted the two great love commands: loving God with our whole being and loving our neighbours as ourselves. The Sermon on the Mount is his great elaboration of that double theme. It is Jesus' fullest account of the ethics of the kingdom of heaven, his own manifesto for a radical discipleship that implicates every aspect of life. The credibility of the church needs urgent restoration. We must not only guard the gospel, we must be seen to live it.

Two words sum up the experience of writing this book: exhilarating and exacting. Nothing could be more thrilling to a Bible student than to devote time to the study of Jesus' Great Sermon. In the extravagant simplicity of the ideals he unreservedly champions, in the noble demands of purity of heart and self-giving love, to drink in Jesus' teaching is to savour a foretaste of heaven. Iona has long been described as a 'thin place', where the distance between earth and heaven seems very slight. In that sense we could describe Jesus' Great Sermon as 'thin words', a sacred summit in the mountain range of inspired Scripture, where the eternal values of the kingdom of heaven press closely upon us.

At the same time, extended study of Jesus' Great Sermon has proved excruciatingly exacting. With every phrase, every messianic intensification, comes a fresh and often painful need for heart-searching and self-examination. If the Sermon is the Everest of discipleship, then with every repeated reading this follower of Jesus has realised ever more clearly how he continues to stumble in the foothills, with a long ascent left to travel.

Because so many wonderful books have been written about the Sermon on the Mount, it could reasonably be asked whether there is room for any more. This book has been spurred into print by several factors: by a love affair with the Great Sermon of more than twenty years that has resulted in my study shelves containing more books on this portion of Scripture than any other; by the kindness and encouragement with which my Bible readings on the Sermon on the Mount were received at Spring Harvest in 1997, especially by one couple who stayed in Skegness a second week in order to hear the teaching again; by the persuasive and supportive skills of Richard Herkes and Jennifer Oldroyd of Kingsway, who believed in the value of a companion volume to my study of the Ten Commandments, so that the two books might speak together to Western society and the Western church; above all, I have been sustained by an inner conviction that every generation has a duty to interpret and apply the demands of discipleship into their new context.

My prayer is, therefore, that this book will help to rekindle a passion for costly discipleship and reinvigorate the 2,000-year-old conviction that local churches are called to live as outposts or colonies of heaven. No greater act of worship could be made at the dawn of the new millennium than to offer ourselves afresh as living sacrifices, individually and corporately, and so, through recovering the practical priorities of whole-life discipleship, restore the credibility of the church.

Rob Warner
All Saints' Day, 1997

Introducing
the Great Sermon

I

The Setting of the Sermon on the Mount
Matthew 4:17 – 5:2

The geographical setting

The hills outside Capernaum sweep up gently from the Sea of Galilee. Those who have not had the privilege to visit the Holy Land need to be warned that there is a distinctive tendency to hyperbole built into the idioms of the Greek language at the time of the New Testament. What Greek describes as a city would in modern usage be no more than a small town. What was then called a mountain would be for us no more than a modest hill. The very phrase 'Sermon on the Mount', probably first used by Augustine in his great exploration of Jesus' teaching, is itself misleading. It may suggest snow-capped ridges, precarious precipices, and a group of disciples roped together and shivering among the rocks while Jesus declaimed his new way of living at the mountain's peak. No such summits can be found in the vicinity of Capernaum.

Mountains had long been imbued with a resonant symbolism in Jewish history and spirituality. It was upon Mount Sinai that Moses met with God and received the Ten Commandments. It was upon Mount Zion that Jerusalem, the city of David, was founded. It was upon Mount Carmel that Elijah successfully called down fire from heaven and saw the decisive public humiliation of the Baalite priests. The high hills were a place of divine revelation, divine provision, divine encounter. The symbolism of Jesus' ascent to the hills around Galilee would have been immediately apparent to the Jews of his day, even though these were hills on a modest scale in a region characterised by a natural beauty that is more gentle than severe. At three critical moments in Jesus' ministry Matthew emphasises the symbolism of a mountain location: the Great Sermon (Mt 5–7), the Transfiguration (Mt 17:1–9), and the Great Commission, once again back in the hills of Galilee (Mt 28:16–20).

A short distance around the lakeside from Capernaum the remains of a first-century jetty have been discovered. This was almost certainly the place where the fishermen of the town kept their boats, cleaning their nets in the springs that gushed into the lake in this area. These springs contain high mineral deposits and in modern times they have been diverted away from the lake now that Galilee functions as a natural reservoir that supplies much of the fresh water for the modern nation of Israel. Near this jetty is Tabgha, a small church that commemorates the feeding of the five thousand. Looking down upon the shoreline are some modest hills, providing an excellent view of the jetty area and the lake. These hillsides are fairly steep and the soil is unremittingly stony. The unyielding ground has doggedly resisted cultivation, even though olive and citrus trees can be cultivated successfully just a few hundred metres away. It is not a rugged place, for in springtime the wild flowers bloom in profusion among the stones. Away from the crowds of the lakeside towns and villages, away from the synagogues and markets, and away from the fishermen and farmers, we know that Jesus often enjoyed the quiet stillness of these solitary hills within a short distance from Capernaum as an ideal setting for private prayer. Here was a brief respite from the attentive crowds and their constant petitioning for healing and deliverance.

Jesus' teaching ministry

Before Matthew comes to the Great Sermon, he explains that Jesus' preaching and healing ministry is already established throughout the region. He has called fishermen as his first disciples (4:18–22) and then begun travelling around Galilee, preaching in the local synagogues (4:23). Matthew provides two initial summaries of his ministry. Jesus began to preach: 'Repent, for the kingdom of heaven is near' (4:17); 'preaching the good news of the kingdom, and healing every disease and sickness' (4:23).

Several distinctive characteristics of Jesus' early ministry are immediately apparent. First, *there is a sense of imminence and urgency* – a deep-seated Jewish longing for God's rule to break out upon the face of the earth is beginning to be fulfilled. There is no distinction between 'kingdom of God' in the other Gospels and Matthew's use of 'kingdom of heaven'. Matthew is not highlighting a different emphasis or aspect of Jesus' teaching. He is merely demonstrating his own Jewishness. The Jews had always avoided naming God as a sign of reverence. Matthew, the most Jewish of the Gospels, embraces this tradition by finding a synonym that is true to Jesus' teaching but strenuously avoids any direct use of the name of God.

Jesus is not announcing the imminent establishment of political independence for the nation state of Israel. His proclamation, developing the longing for a new kind of kingdom that had been stirred by the prophets through many generations, is not about political geography and human government. The kingdom of God represents something more profound, subtle and wide ranging than the liberation of the Jews from Roman imperialism. Jesus is describing the prospect of life with an extra dimension. He invites his hearers to live in faithful obedience to the person and ways of their Father in heaven. But this is no impersonal surrender to a distant deity. God's very presence is breaking out upon the face of the earth, so that the disciples of Jesus can experience the rule of God on a daily basis, living out their lives in an environment shot through with the immanence of the living God.

Second, *Jesus' teaching cannot be separated from a call to repentance*. The whole tenor of Jesus is positive and life-affirming. Nothing could be more remote from the life-constricting negativity of the legalistic religious obsessions of the Pharisees. They were forever nit-picking, on the look-out for proof that others were completely in the wrong and abject failures in their endeavours to live for God. Jesus, on the other hand, was always offering a second chance, a fresh start, to the outsiders and failures, the moral outcasts and religious rejects of Jewish society. Jesus' voice resounds with hope and opportunity; his teaching is always an invitation to explore a better way of life. He explained that he was calling people to discover and enjoy life in all its fullness (Jn 10:10).

The Greek word for repentance indicates a U-turn, a 180-degree shift in priorities. Jesus' repeated call to repentance is by no means anti-life, but it does indicate that we are incapable of living the Jesus way if we simply persist in 'doing what comes naturally'. Jesus makes no attempt to pander to his audience, offering them some kind of easy-believism with a religious feel-good factor. His is not the wimpish pseudo-spirituality of the late twentieth century that blandly affirms the best in people without making any ethical demands. Instead, Jesus' call to repentance urges his followers not to minor adjustments in their trajectory through life, but to a comprehensive, rigorous and continuing life reappraisal. According to Jesus, we cannot even begin to discover the life of the kingdom of heaven without recognising the absolute necessity of personal repentance. 'I did it my way' may have become the anthem of late twentieth-century values, in a society that pursues individualism and DIY morality, but the kingdom of heaven has a very different point of entry. We have to be prepared to renounce living 'my way' and endeavour to start walking in the Jesus way.

Third, *Jesus' teaching is about the present as well as the future.* The fullness of the kingdom of heaven has not only drawn very near, but according to Jesus the rule of God is already breaking out in the present. In response to the urgent call to repentance, people are beginning to enter a new dimension of living in surrender to God. Here Jesus is emulating the great tradition of the Hebrew prophets. As they prophesied about the future, there were always present implications, an invitation to avert judgement through repentance or to hasten the fulfilment of God's promises through active and faithful obedience. Theologians have coined the phrase 'partially realised eschatology' to seek to express this temporal overlap in Jesus' teaching. The term eschatology signifies teaching about the last days, the dawn of the end of time, from the Greek word *eschaton*, meaning end. A futurist eschatology explores far-off days, remote from the present generation. A realised eschatology concentrates entirely on the present, proposing that these are the last days in their entirety and fullness – there is nothing more to look forward to, for what we see is all that we are ever going to get. A partially realised eschatology recognises that something new has begun but it is not yet complete. There is a now dimension – we are invited to run the risks of radical discipleship yielding to and experiencing God's rule in the present – but there is simultaneously a not-yet dimension where the kingdom has come and yet is still coming; the end times have begun, but in their fullness they have not yet been consummated.

This now-and-not-yet tension is found throughout the New Testament. For example, Paul speaks of the Holy Spirit as the firstfruits (Rom 8:23), which indicates that while the Spirit has now been made available in the new way the Old

Testament prophets had promised, the full harvest of heaven is yet to be enjoyed. The source of this creative tension, this temporal overlap in which we can enter a preliminary and partial participation in our future hope, is an unmistakable part of Jesus' teaching from the earliest days of his public ministry.

Fourth, *the proclamation of the kingdom is accompanied by miracles*. The eruption of God's rule in the present, the inbreaking of the future hope, is demonstrated and experienced in Jesus' healing and deliverance ministry. There is nothing gratuitous about Jesus' miracles, no hovering one metre above the ground for twenty minutes to demonstrate his divinity. He is forever demonstrating the power of divine love in action. The liberating, life-affirming rule of God overcomes the destructive power of sickness and death. The same divine authority unmasks the tyranny of demonic infiltration and expels the demons from their human hosts. According to the Gospels it is quite impossible to sever Jesus' teaching from his miracles. They are woven together seamlessly into a single ministry. Jesus is no mere wonder-worker, an itinerant healer providing spectacular demonstrations of rare and mysterious supernatural powers. Nor is he merely a profound moral teacher, providing wise yet demanding ethical insights without reference to the supernatural. The healing ministry and the call to a new lifestyle are expressed in a creative integration, and always with the common thread of the inbreaking of the rule of God.

The fringes of Christianity have often been plagued by self-styled wonder workers whose public ministry is devoid of biblical teaching. Sometimes, still worse, their claimed miraculous successes provide a spurious legitimacy for idle or even heretical speculation, whether ignorant or wanton, with the claim: I have the power, so what I say must be right. Within the learned portals of religious respectability, the traditional church is more typically plagued by the opposite excess: highly informed ethical pontification, devoid of any appetite for spiritual power. Just as those with an instinctive yearning for the spectacular can despise the life of the mind, the learned often have no time for the supernatural – it seems so vulgar, so disorderly. Jesus deftly avoids both extremes, both pigeon holes. He is no exponent of tabloid miracles, full of sensationalism but devoid of all content. Nor can his teaching and enactment of the coming of the kingdom of God be confined within the straitjacket of post-Enlightenment rationalism. Jesus' approach is reasonable but not rationalistic. He makes logical and persuasively argued appeals to the rational mind, but he brings with him the supernatural presence and rule of God that are ultimately beyond human understanding.

The miracles that are integral to the coming of the kingdom and to Jesus' ministry are also non-coercive. They are 'signs', to use the favourite term of John's Gospel, actions that point beyond themselves to the ultimate and eternal significance of Jesus. Their full meaning can only be grasped from the perspective of faith, but while they may promote faith they cannot compel it. Although some saw in his miracles the definitive and divine confirmation of Jesus' spiritual authority, others found fault with the same healings, explaining them away or even suggesting that it was Satan who had endowed Jesus with supernatural power (Mt 12:24).

Those who suggest that a greater frequency of divine healing would spontaneously and automatically promote church growth or even revival across the Western world have not read their New Testament very carefully. Even in the time of Jesus, the most dramatic and compelling of miracles provoked a threefold reaction: some believed and rejoiced in Jesus' supernatural authority; some dismissed the miracles and rejected the wonder-worker; others were unable to get beyond a sense of mystery and ambiguity, accepting that something inexplicable and possibly super-natural seemed to be happening, without being able to come to any definite conclusions.

Fifth, *Jesus' own identity and role are integral to his teaching about the kingdom of God.* The distinctive quality of Jesus' teaching is apparent in comparison with John the Baptist. John presented himself as a herald of the Greater One who would come after him. He declared his message faithfully, but he always and rigorously kept himself distinct from it. So far as John was concerned, if he remained the centre of attention for his hearers, he would have failed completely as a preacher. Not so for Jesus. He does far more than proclaim his message, embody his teaching in his lifestyle and demonstrate a supernatural authority in his healing ministry. People are not only invited to respond to God, but to Jesus himself. He speaks with the authority of God; he casts out demons by the 'finger of God' (Lk 11:20); his call to discipleship is not in the third person but the first – not simply 'Follow God', but 'Follow me'. Jesus does not merely announce the coming of the kingdom of God. He brings it. The man becomes the message.

The crowds and the disciples

Jesus' preaching ministry began in the synagogues of the Galilean region, but soon the people begin to gather around Jesus wherever he goes, both to hear his teaching and to bring their most desperate medical and spiritual casualties to him, in hope of healing and deliverance. At first the news spreads throughout Syria, then the crowds begin to gather from Galilee, Decapolis – the region of the ten cities – Jerusalem, Judea and the region to the east of the River Jordan (Mt 4:23–25).

The press of the crowds has become ever more demand-ing, and so the scene is set for the Great Sermon. Faced once again with large numbers of people, Jesus moves up onto the hillside (or mountainside if we translate more literally the habitual hyperbole of the original Greek). Usually the hills are a place of withdrawal where Jesus goes for solitary prayer or where he takes a few selected disciples. However, on this occasion Matthew reports that Jesus ascended the hillside and then sat down. Those who love fell-walking know what it is to reach a summit, often soaked in sweat, and then enjoy the sheer pleasure of sitting, or sometimes collapsing, relishing the sense of achievement as you take in the view. However, Jesus' choice of posture is less to do with aching limbs than rabbinic tradition, for among the Jews the custom was that someone about to teach would sit down as a way of announcing his intention. We see this same posture in the synagogue at Nazareth where Jesus preached for the first time after his baptism. He stood to read from Isaiah, but then sat down before beginning to speak (Lk 4:16, 20–21).

Jesus' intention was plain to his disciples, for Matthew records that they responded by coming to him and then he launched into his teaching. When Jesus sat down, therefore, he must have still been visible from the level ground by the lakeside. If he had continued to ascend away from the crowds until he was lost from view, no one would have been able to interpret his sitting down as a clear indication that now was a time not for solitary withdrawal, but for momentous preaching. Even as Moses had ascended the mountain to receive God's revelation of the Ten Commandments, the disciples ascended the hillside to receive the teaching of Jesus.

So how many heard the Great Sermon? There is an ambiguity in Matthew's account. Jesus sees a large crowd and ascends the hillside (5:1). But only his disciples then come to him (5:1). However, at the end of the Sermon those who have an amazed response to the authority of his teaching are 'the crowds' (7:28–29). Some scholars marginalise these details as 'mere redactional material' – that is, they are viewed as Matthew's editorial bridges between his source materials, potentially informative in terms of Matthew's distinctive perspective and themes, but of no historical value or significance.

There is no justification for a hasty or casual dismissal of such details, but before considering them further we need first to recognise the significance of the word 'disciple'. The word is common in all three Synoptic Gospels, but Matthew uses the term far more often (seventy-six times, compared to Mark's fifty-seven and Luke's forty-five), frequently in contexts without any parallel in the other Synoptics. The Greek word for 'disciple' signifies a learner or student. In the Jewish tradition, a rabbi's followers were to learn not only from his words but from his life. Disciples of Jesus can therefore be said to be those who choose to submit and devote themselves to the wisdom and lifestyle of their chosen teacher. Matthew emphasises the meaning of discipleship through several details: the original disciples are directly called by Jesus to become his followers (4:18–22); true disciples do the will of the Father and are closer to Jesus than his blood relations (12:46–50); the secrets of the kingdom are given to the disciples, who understand more deeply than the casual listeners among the people (13:10–11). Nonetheless, the disciples are not glamorised, for Jesus frequently refers to them as those with 'little faith' (6:30; 8:26; 14:31; 16:8). In their unvarnished fallibility the disciples become foils for the untarnished perfection of their Master.

The fullest definition of discipleship on Jesus' lips is found in the Great Commission, with which Matthew concludes his Gospel.

Then Jesus came to them and said, 'All authority in heaven and on earth has been given to me. Therefore go and make disciples of all nations, baptising them in the name of the Father and of the Son and of the Holy Spirit, and teaching them to obey everything I have commanded you. And surely I am with you always, to the very end of the age.' (Mt 28:18–20)

The disciples will now be drawn from all ethnic groupings and not just the Jews. They will be *baptised* in the name of the Trinity and *instructed* in Jesus' teaching. They will *seek to obey* their Master in everything, *experience the risen Christ's continuing presence*, and in turn will *become disciple-makers*. The multiplication of disciples is meant to become a continuing, even the defining, priority of the followers of Christ.

Within his narrative, Matthew frequently uses two terms that encapsulate the essential nature of discipleship. In the introduction to the Great Sermon, the disciples 'came to' Jesus. This verb is used fifty-two times by Matthew, compared with six by Mark and eleven by Luke, and is clearly used to express a continuing desire for closeness to Jesus. The second verb that Matthew uses frequently is 'follow'. The usage originates in Jesus' habitual phrase in his repeated call to discipleship: 'Follow me' (4:19; 8:22; 9:9; 10:38; 16:24; 19:21). In the calling of the first disciples, they left their nets and 'followed him' (Mt 4:20, 22). Similarly, when Matthew the tax collector was called, he 'got up and followed him' (9:9). When Jesus summed up the life of a disciple, the verb is used once again: 'If anyone would come after me, he must deny himself and take up his cross and follow me' (Mt 16:24). The same description is central to Peter's definition of the cost and practice of discipleship: 'Peter answered him, "We have left everything to follow you!"' (Mt 19:27).

Matthew frequently describes crowds as 'following' Jesus (4:25; 8:1; 12:15; 14:13; 19:2; 20:29), and some who were healed by Jesus also 'followed' him (20:34). After his arrest, Peter 'followed' him at a distance (26:58), and the women who stood in vigil near the cross had 'followed' him from

Galilee to care for his needs (27:55). Matthew further reinforces the central importance of following Jesus by using the verb in settings where it is deliberately artificial and contrived. After the Great Sermon, Jesus came down from the hillside and great crowds 'followed him'(8:1), which almost suggests that they descended in his footsteps. When Jesus got into a boat, his disciples 'followed him' (8:23), so that their method of embarkation becomes expressive of their devoted discipleship. Such is Matthew's emphatic Christ-centredness that even in the incidental details of his narrative he continually underlines the need to come to Jesus in pursuit of intimacy with the Master, and also to keep on following closely wherever he may lead, in determined, practical and costly obedience.

At first sight there were just two audiences for Jesus' teaching: the disciples and the crowds; the followers and those whose interest in Jesus was more casual and passing. On this basis, it would seem that Jesus must have left the crowd in their entirety at the foot of the mountain, with the result that only the privileged few were entitled to hear the Great Sermon. We must, however, allow for a greater fluidity and overlap between these two groupings. While the original disciples continued to travel with Jesus, during the years of Jesus' travelling ministry others must have presumably decided to commit themselves to following him, whether they joined his travelling group or chose to stay behind in the communities where they lived. This suggests that there may have been two kinds of disciple: those called by Jesus as part of the original travelling team and those who were gradually added to their number. This in turn creates the possibility that there were two kinds of crowd: the casual, impulsive mass of people for whom Jesus is no more than a passing celebrity; and a smaller, inner crowd of emerging disciples, who are growing into the convictions and commitment of living faith.

Two further groups of disciples are implicitly referred to throughout Matthew's Gospel. First, the disciples of Matthew's own generation, particularly those in the church or region for whom his Gospel was originally written. For them, the actual disciples of the time of Jesus have come to represent and typify what it means to be a follower of the Master. But Matthew's fellow disciples are by no means the end of the line. All generations of disciples are called to be disciple-makers, and in Matthew's Gospel the foundational disciples explore the meaning of living discipleship, not only for Matthew's own generation, but for every succeeding generation. The original disciples are at one and the same time both historically specific as real individuals and yet representatives of the believing response in every generation to Jesus' timeless and universal call to discipleship.

Reconstructing the setting

We are nearly ready to suggest a reconstruction of the original setting for the Great Sermon, but first we must consider two more issues: how Matthew's Sermon on the Mount is related to Luke's Sermon on the Plain (Lk 6:17–49), and the actual nature of the material that Matthew presents as a single sermon.

Luke's Sermon on the Plain has several fundamental differences from Matthew's Great Sermon. In terms of the contents, the most striking differences are that Luke's account is much shorter, it contains four blessings and four woes compared with Matthew's eight blessings and no corresponding woes, and Luke's account of Jesus' teaching on prayer is recorded separately (11:1–13). Topographically, Luke's sermon is given on a level place, Matthew's on the mount.

It is not difficult to reconcile these two accounts. We can identify many 'level places' in Galilee, not only beside the lake, but also up among the hills. Such a place need not be imagined as a remote plateau among high mountains, for the gentle hills of Galilee near Capernaum actually provide many level places, enfolded by hillsides, that would serve well as natural amphitheatres for open-air preaching.

As to the contents, neither Gospel makes any claim to provide a verbatim account of Jesus' preaching. Matthew's much longer record can be read aloud in less than fifteen minutes, so it is natural to conclude that we have no more than a summary of the key points of Jesus' teaching. Anyone who has compared lecture or sermon notes with someone else in the same audience will have discovered that two people can record and recall someone's public speaking with quite different emphases. It is therefore quite plausible to suggest that Matthew and Luke are reporting the same event, but from significantly different perspectives. This would mean that they are relying on different eyewitness accounts passed on in verbal or written traditions. They may also have chosen to edit the material in different ways, making different selections from their sources rather than attempting an absolutely exhaustive account of the teaching of Jesus.

Such a reconciliation of the two accounts is plausible, but not strictly necessary. All itinerant preachers will know that more or less the same message can often be delivered in more than one place. It was Spurgeon who observed that if a sermon is worth preaching once it is worth preaching more than once. Such repetition is often inexact: one section from a message may be repeated in a different context; an effective illustration may be used with a new emphasis to bring home a different point. As Jesus travelled among the lakeside communities and throughout Galilee it seems reasonable to suppose that he would sometimes repeat and even develop his parables and often return to teaching about his key themes such as forgiveness and prayer, repentance and the kingdom of God. Therefore, although Luke may be recording the same sermon from a different perspective, it seems at least equally plausible that he is recording a different, but similar, sermon from Jesus' itinerant preaching. If that is the case, it should come as no surprise to find many parallels, both verbal and thematic, alongside significant variations in emphasis.

Two other theories about the nature of the Great Sermon should be considered briefly. Some have proposed that this sermon, as a single, coherent statement of Jesus' essential teaching on discipleship, has been invented by Matthew. It is as if someone found a box of jigsaw pieces that came from several different puzzles, and forced a great number of them into a new and artificial combination. That is, the verbal or written traditions upon which Matthew drew may have only contained the most memorable individual sayings and fragments of Jesus' teaching, and from these he has reconstructed a representative sermon, reliable in its individual details but probably never preached by Jesus in this particular form.

The weakness of this theory is that too little can be proved; too much is speculation. We have no direct access to any earlier verbal tradition in order to make a conclusive comparison with Matthew's account. And if there was an early written source upon which Matthew – or Matthew and Luke – drew for his distinctive material, it has been lost for ever. What we can say for sure is that the gospel writers all agree that Jesus was renowned not only for his memorable short sayings and his unforgettable parables, but also for his extended preaching, and Matthew and Luke both provide an example of this preaching, whether or not they are reporting the identical message given on the same occasion. If it could be proved somehow that the Great Sermon was a later assemblage of the collected fragments of Jesus' teaching, that would not diminish the timeless and inexhaustible profundity of his words. However, the lack of any conclusive evidence that the Great Sermon is Matthew's invention, in which authentic sayings of Jesus have been artificially arranged and connected, encourages us to trust Matthew and Luke as faithful, but not verbatim, reporters of the extended preaching of Jesus.

As an intermediate position between a later assemblage of isolated fragments and the summary of a single sermon, some have suggested that the teaching of the Great Sermon is so rich, so demanding, that it may represent the notes taken not from a single message but from an interconnected series. Perhaps Jesus provided a Galilean summer school in discipleship (a kind of Keswick or Spring Harvest by the Sea). That is, the Great Sermon represents a preaching series in the hills held over several days, during which people from the crowds had an opportunity gradually to make the transition into committed discipleship. This theory is suggestive and intriguing. It allows us to imagine the people choosing to leave their work and home for a fixed number of days in order to drink in the teaching of Jesus. It does however have two major weaknesses. First, the Gospels never indicate the possibility of such a summer school. That does not mean such an event could not possibly have happened, but it reduces the likelihood. Second, the very concept of an organised summer school probably has more to do with twentieth-century Western culture, pre-planned and diarised, than with the more impulsive immediacy of first-century Galilean peasantry.

We are now able to reconstruct the setting for the Great Sermon. Jesus was faced with a large crowd, many of whom were more interested in his wonder-working than his call to repentance and invitation to respond to the coming of the kingdom of God. Knowing that the time had come to provide fuller teaching for those who were serious about living as his disciples, Jesus determined to stride vigorously up the hillside. At first it looked as if Jesus wanted to be alone. However, where the hillside began to level out Jesus suddenly stopped and then made a point of sitting down while in full view of the crowds below. The signal was unmistakable. This was not a day when Jesus was going to devote his energies to the sick and demonised; but for those who were prepared to make the effort to clamber up the hillside, the Teacher had some important, even momentous, instructions that he wanted to deliver to all who were willing to be counted among his followers.

The first to ascend were Jesus' closest disciples. As soon as they were confident that Jesus wanted their company, they began to climb the hill. Gradually the crowd began to divide. Since Jesus was offering a day devoted to preaching, some decided they would be better off returning promptly to their homes and work. Others were more serious about learning from Jesus and so they too began to climb. Many were not able to get near to Jesus. Perhaps some were not even able to get onto the level ground, but rested where they could on the steep ground of the hillside, and where the natural amphitheatre of the hills meant they could still hear his unforgettable words. When Jesus finished preaching, this was the crowd who expressed amazement at his authority – not the people left behind at the lakeside, but those outside the inner circle who were beginning to make the move towards committed discipleship. Although they were not part of Jesus' travelling band, many were still clear about one thing: they had decided to count themselves among the followers of Jesus.

2

The Intentions of the Sermon on the Mount

The setting in Matthew's Gospel

In order to have the fullest appreciation of the Great Sermon, we not only need to understand something of its place in Jesus' ministry and his original target audience, we also need to explore the significance of its setting within the structure of Matthew's Gospel. The conventions of biographical writing in the modern West mean that most biographies provide a chronological account of their subject's life. Such an approach was extremely rare in the ancient world, where a life study was more likely to be organised thematically. Only Luke makes a specific claim to provide a chronological account of Jesus' life, and he emphasises his particular approach as something unusual and distinctive: 'Therefore since I myself have carefully investigated everything from the beginning, it seemed good also to me to write an orderly account' (Lk 1:3).

Furthermore, modern biographies usually treat death briefly, concentrating on the life phases of greatest productivity and significance, whereas the Gospels devote about one third of their length to Jesus' last week before death and then his resurrection. Jesus' crucifixion is not portrayed as a tragic and premature accident or defeat, but rather as the decisive, purposeful and celebrated climax of his life.

Matthew contains 90 per cent of Mark, which is one of the indicators that has resulted in the consensus that Mark was the first written Gospel, subsequently used as a resource by Matthew and Luke. Matthew's extra material, in comparison with Mark, can be found in particular in the opening genealogy, the infancy narratives, sayings of Jesus and additional resurrection narratives. The broad outline of the geographical structure is similar to Mark's: early ministry in Galilee, a short and transitional travel section (Mt 19–20), and the final period of ministry, death and resurrection in Jerusalem.

Matthew is the most Jewish of the Gospels, which presumably reflects the author's personal concerns and background, and may also indicate a Jewish Christian setting for his distinctive portrayal of Jesus. The opening genealogy, which echoes those of the Old Testament, begins by stating Jesus' two most important earthly ancestors: Abraham, which affirms that he is a true Jew, and David, which is the first indicator that Jesus is the promised Messiah. Matthew frequently repeats the title 'Son of David' in order to emphasise this messianic theme (9:27; 12:23; 15:22; 20:30–31; 21:9, 15; 22:42). He repeatedly quotes the Old Testament to demonstrate prophetic fulfilment at key moments of Jesus' life (the virgin birth, the flight to Egypt, the massacre in Bethlehem, settling in Nazareth, the move to Capernaum, the healing ministry, messianic secrecy, teaching in parables, the entry into Jerusalem and the betrayal and burial of Judas). He also regularly employs a distinctively Jewish phrase to describe the Hebrew scriptures – 'the law and the prophets' – and includes a series of sayings in which Jesus explains that his own ministry is specifically directed towards his fellow Jews (10:5–6; 15:24) and denounces Israel's official leaders as failed shepherds (9:36; 23:1–36).

As to Matthew's literary structure, it can be analysed in two ways. First, the Gospel presents itself in three distinct sections: the person of Jesus (1:1 – 4:16), the public ministry of Jesus (4:17 – 16:20) and finally Jesus' trial, death and resurrection (16:21 – 28:20). At the start of the second and third sections, Matthew uses the same introductory phrase: 'from that time'. Although this is a simple structural sub-division of the Gospel, it provides a very limited interpretative framework and adds little to our understanding of Matthew's distinctive approach and themes.

The primary structure of Matthew is immediately apparent and much more interesting, for the Gospel is composed of alternate blocks of teaching and action. Just as Shakespeare's tragedies often juxtapose scenes of intense emotion with scenes of comic relief, Matthew develops his portrait of Jesus through contrasting sections where different kinds of material are gathered, not for comic relief but for separating out the two essential aspects of Jesus' public ministry. There are five teaching blocks: the Great Sermon (5–7), sending out the Twelve (10), parables of the kingdom (13), teaching on the church (18), and finally judgements on the Pharisees and teaching on the end times (23–25). At the end of each of these sections Matthew uses a similar bridging phrase to the next action section: 'When Jesus had finished saying these things . . .'

In contrast with Mark's Gospel, which concentrates on Jesus as a man of action, Matthew's way of organising his material throws the spotlight upon Christ the Teacher. The immediate impression is that Jesus' life is shaped around a series of long sermons, punctuated by periods in which he travelled, healed and cast out demons. For Jewish readers these five blocks of teaching would carry an extra resonance. They would instantly recognise an understated but suggestive parallel with the opening five books of the Old Testament, traditionally ascribed to Moses. Here, by implication, is a new Pentateuch, revelatory teaching of a new way of living by one who is greater than Moses.

While Matthew's structure implicitly conveys Jesus' superiority to Moses, we should not overstate the force of this comparison. It is certainly conveyed by the structure, but it remains more implicit than explicit. The 'greater than Moses' theme is not developed or emphasised by Matthew, nor is it plausible to attempt to develop any detailed similarities or equivalence between the individual speeches in Matthew and the sequence of books in the Pentateuch. What is pivotal to Matthew is not the implicit parallel with Moses, but his explicit structural emphasis that Jesus is the greatest Teacher and Preacher the world has ever known.

Matthew's Gospel comes to a resounding crescendo with the climax of the Great Commission. The risen Christ has returned from Jerusalem to Galilee for his final words of instruction to the infant church. Now it is the original disciples who are called to become teachers – 'teaching them to obey everything I have commanded you' (28:20). The great climax of the Gospel of Christ the Teacher moves in two complementary directions. First, it directs the original disciples, and through them the disciples of Matthew's church and in every succeeding generation, to be outward looking, seeking to make new disciples of all peoples in the continuing mission of the church.

At the same time, with an emphatic phrase – 'teaching them to obey everything I have commanded you' (Mt 28:20), Jesus' final words direct every generation of disciples back into the contents of Matthew's book. The Great Commission spells out the enduring principle that at the very heart of discipleship is knowing Jesus and seeking to put his teaching into practice. Matthew's Gospel, through its literary structure and dominant themes, therefore presents itself not only as a life of Jesus, but also as a handbook for all of Jesus' continuing disciples, initially but by no means exclusively for Jewish Christians in churches known to Matthew, who aspired to be part of an effective disciple-making church. Since discipleship comprises an overarching theme and purpose of the entire Gospel, it is beyond dispute that the Sermon on the Mount is absolutely pivotal to Matthew's concerns. Here is the first great block of Jesus' teaching, given, along with the Great Commission, a particular structural prominence. Here is found the essence of practical and radical Christian obedience. Here is nothing less than Jesus' own manual of discipleship.

Interpreting the Sermon

When the demands of the Sermon are so great, it should hardly come as a surprise that many interpreters have found ingenious ways of establishing why it does not apply to their generation. The contrast with the Ten Commandments could not be more striking. Far from being in any sense arbitrary or wilful, the Commandments encapsulate the moral order that is intrinsic to human existence. They are a brilliant, succinct summary of the foundational moral values that are needed to establish and maintain a civilised society. In short, the Ten Commandments make obvious and practical good sense. The Sermon on the Mount, by contrast, is an ethic of extremism. Jesus' demands are positively mountainous and his idealism may appear naive and unworkable. The focus is no longer outward conformity to a universal moral framework, but an inner dedication to the ways of Jesus, arising from the hidden life of the heart and character.

We can begin by identifying several interpretations that are simply mistaken. First, there have been occasional, bizarre attempts to turn the ethics of the Sermon into a new law, imposed upon some kind of evangelical utopia. But Jesus' teaching is supremely unenforceable – its concern is purity of heart and self-giving love. On the rare occasions when Christians have attempted to legislate the demands of the Sermon, the result has been failure and usually disaster. As public law the Sermon just does not work.

Three further interpretations go to the opposite extreme. Rather than seeking to impose the ethic of Jesus upon society, they suggest that even Christians can conveniently ignore Jesus' extravagant demands. Second, some suggest that the Sermon presents an interim ethic, restricted to the period of Jesus' earthly life, which is no longer appropriate in the new age that has begun with his death and resurrection. Third, others restrict the demands of the Sermon to the other end of the Christian era, suggesting that this ethic will only apply after the Second Coming (or shortly before, depending upon whether the eschatology is pre- or post-millennial). Fourth, still others suggest that the Sermon on the Mount applies only to an élite, to the crack troops of the original disciples, and perhaps in addition to the exceptionally devout, the saints and heroes among later generations of believers.

These three interpretations are fatally flawed by a crucial omission from the text of Matthew's Gospel. If the Great Sermon's relevance was restricted to the first generation, the last generation or an ethical élite, then surely Jesus would have made the narrow focus of its application absolutely plain and unambiguous. What's more, Matthew's understanding of the continuing importance of the Sermon is unmistakable in the literary structure of his Gospel. If Jesus' teaching remained the authoritative manual of discipleship for Matthew's generation, then its authority should logically remain undiminished for all succeeding generations of Christian disciples. Without an explicit clause of exception, it is simply not plausible to claim that Jesus' demands were never intended to apply to subsequent generations of believers.

The next three accounts each make a valuable point, but provide a less than complete interpretation. Fifth, the Great

Sermon is an extended and extraordinary self-description of the most exceptional of men. There have been great and wise moral philosophers whose personal lives have failed to measure up to their own ideals. But in the case of Jesus there is a remarkable and comprehensive consonance between principles and practice. What he taught is what he was. The moral idealism of his preaching found full expression and embodiment in his life and character. The fit is perfect. The teaching sums up the man.

Sixth, the Sermon presents an impossible ideal that brings home our desperate need for a Saviour. From time to time I meet people who explain that, although they do not consider themselves to be in any sense religious, they nonetheless accept that Jesus was a great moral teacher, and as for the Sermon on the Mount, they live by it. The most generous conclusion that can possibly be drawn is that it must be some time since they last read Jesus' words! Far from setting before us a readily achievable set of moral standards, Jesus' teaching calls us to such heights of inner purity and self-giving love that they lead the earnest reader not towards self-satisfied complacency, but rather to despair. No one in their right mind can explore Jesus' words and honestly claim that in their own life these standards are kept to the full.

Seventh, the Sermon demands a personal response. As with all Jesus' proclamation, his hearers were implicated rather than entertained. And the response that Jesus invites is not simply to a set of ideas, but to his own person. He is the one who brings the kingdom of God. He is the one who teaches the highest and most demanding ethic ever expressed on the face of the earth. He is the one who totally fulfils and embodies the ethic and the coming of the kingdom of God. Always his life and teaching provoke ultimate questions: Who is this man, and how should we respond to him?

An eighth response fully accepts the insights of the fifth, sixth and seventh, but then takes things further. Jesus certainly provides a self-description that exposes our inadequacies and need of a Saviour, and therefore demands a response of faith. But he is also addressing his disciples with practical teaching that has immense and unavoidable implications for every aspect of life. The ethic of the kingdom of God is not the means to salvation, a path that we must first walk in our own resources in order to win God's approval. Nor is it a body of teaching that can be fully understood or enacted in detachment from the Great Teacher. Once we have put our trust in Jesus the Messiah, the Sermon on the Mount presents and explains the ideals of the lifestyle that flows from personal faith. Jesus' Great Sermon always beckons us onwards, inviting us to continue to ascend the mountainous pathway that leads to the demanding and rigorous heights of true and living discipleship.

PART ONE

The Way of Fulfilment
Matthew 5:3–16

3

The Search for Fulfilment –
Discovering the Beatitudes
Matthew 5:3–12

Every society has its own ideas about the keys to happiness and success. Jesus' Great Sermon begins with eight qualities that together make possible life to the full, and secure the blessing of God. The Beatitudes of Jesus follow a regular pattern. Each begins with the standard declaration of blessedness, a particular positive quality is named, and then the statement is completed by naming the benefit connected with each virtue. The eightfold repetition of the word 'blessed' is emphatic. Here is both description and promise – an account of the kind of life that will prove the most rewarding, and an assurance that God's favour will come upon those who adopt such a lifestyle.

'Blessed' is a word with a number of meanings. The word can simply mean 'happy', which is how it has been translated in some modern English versions. In recent Greek Cypriot history there was a church leader whose name was the same Greek word – Archbishop Makarios – although 'happy' hardly summed up his public image in the Western media! 'Happy' speaks of an emotional condition: positive and pleasant, but by its very nature both passing and superficial. 'Happy' is woefully inadequate to express the heart of Jesus' promise. 'Blessed' is a more precise translation, with the limitation that the word is rarely used these days and has therefore become rather vague. In traditional English usage, 'Bless you' is a polite response when someone has just sneezed. This idiom goes back to the Middle Ages, when sneezing was one of the early symptoms of the Plague. The word was therefore used in inauspicious circumstances in order to attempt to ward off the prospect of death. In much modern American usage, 'I'm really blessed' no longer signifies a close call with the Black Death, but has come to indicate material prosperity and an easy passage through life. Neither of these usages gives us adequate clues to Jesus' meaning.

When the Gospel writers sum up Jesus' preaching, they consistently use phrases along the lines of 'The kingdom of God is near. Repent and believe' (Mt 4:17; Mk 1:15). The present availability of God's ruling presence is inextricably linked to the practical ethics of Jesus. Loving one another is thoroughly integrated with loving God. Jesus' concern in the Beatitudes is not merely to describe an emotional condition, and is certainly not to provide some kind of guarantee of material prosperity or a high quotient of the feel-good factor. What he describes and promises is a new standing before God for those who embrace his ethic of self-giving love. To be 'blessed', in the context and meaning of Jesus' Beatitudes, is to live in the confidence that God's favour is resting upon us.

Irrespective of outward circumstances or our inner emotional condition, Jesus proposes that it is possible to live in the confidence that we are under the favour of God. Of course such a privileged status is liable to make us happy at least from time to time, but while the feelings of happiness may come and go, the status of divine blessedness remains stable and secure. Our blessedness is assured not by personal circumstances nor by feelings, but by divine decree. Jesus gives us no direct explanation within the Beatitudes as to how to enter this condition of blessedness. But he certainly indicates that such blessing is a newly unveiled aspect of reality that has become available in the inbreaking of the kingdom of heaven and can therefore become an integral component of our present spiritual experience.

The eight characteristics do not represent eight different kinds of person. Rather, they connect together to define a single, comprehensive state of blessedness. In the same way that the fruit of the Spirit is meant to be cultivated in all its aspects, rather than choosing one or two personal favourites from the bunch, the implication is not that it will be sufficient if we seek to pursue any one or two of the Beatitudes, but rather that we should endeavour, as individuals, households and communities of disciples, to seek after the first seven and not be surprised if they are followed by the eighth, namely persecution.

There is clearly some sort of interconnectedness between the Beatitudes. John Chrysostom, a gloriously gifted Bible teacher of the early church, spoke of them as a 'golden chain'. The Beatitudes are supremely Jesus' self-description – together they represent the finest summary of both the character and the blessedness of Christ himself. But is there also a sequence? Some have tried to suggest that the first four are directed vertically towards God, the rest horizontally towards men and women. On more careful examination, this categorisation is artificial and contrived. In particular, the third, celebrating meekness, is directed both vertically and horizontally, as is the sixth, celebrating purity of heart. Perhaps the most we can say about the orientation of the Beatitudes is that, like Jesus' summary of the Law, they explore simultaneously and connectedly our relationships both with God and with one another.

Others have proposed that the Beatitudes represent a ladder of ascending virtue, as if we graduate from one level of blessedness to the next. Once again we have to respond that this is an over-simplification. To construct a rigid sequence or hierarchy within the Beatitudes is to mishandle them, misunderstanding the kind of teaching that Jesus provides. The connections are more poetic than mathematical, more allusive than a strictly logical progression.

This poetic quality is highly significant. The Beatitudes provoke more questions than they answer. With a haunting beauty they commend and explore a startlingly different approach to life. But they remain allusive and mysterious, evoking and intending to inspire a spiritual and moral revolution, while declining to put too much flesh on the bones. A political programme spells out a specific response to a particular set of social and economic circumstances. It is constrained in space and time so that the more precisely relevant the policies are to present-day circumstances, the more likely that they will seem dated ten years later, let alone two thousand. Jesus' words, by contrast, lay out the terrain of the kingdom of God and the promised state of blessedness in a style that is deliberately timeless and universal. His followers are left to work out the practical implications for themselves in their own distinctive life setting.

What is beyond dispute is that Jesus provides a resounding affirmation for some generally unpopular and less than appreciated attitudes and circumstances. Poverty, mourning and meekness are gateways to spiritual blessing, when normally they would be considered disadvantageous, weak or even negative conditions of life. Even persecution becomes a privilege and something to be embraced willingly, when normal instincts of self-preservation would prompt us to avoid such a prospect at all costs.

This gives the Beatitudes an unexpected, subversive quality, overturning what are normally understood to be the givens of good fortune and a happy life. In a memorable phrase, one Anabaptist writer described this inversion of normal expectations and values as the 'upside down kingdom'. Jesus calls us to a discipleship that is constantly full of surprises and requires an altogether new outlook, far from the cautious conventions of respectable human religion, ancient or modern. Here is a new way of living, a new perspective on what matters most in life. The customs and priorities of this world are questioned, overthrown and even reversed by the higher calling of the kingdom of heaven.

Jesus' Beatitudes certainly constitute a set of virtues more honoured in the breach than in the remembrance. If we begin from the prevailing virtues of our society we can easily construct an alternative collection of Beatitudes that has become normative today:

Blessed are the wealthy
  because theirs is the Dow Jones Index.
Blessed are those who enjoy a good party
  because they will drown their sorrows.
Blessed are the assertive,
  for they will get to the top of their career.
Blessed are those who hunger and thirst after chemical stimulation,
  for designer drugs are more widely available with
  every passing year.
Blessed are the ruthless
  because no one will get in their way.
Blessed are the cold of heart,
  for they won't get hurt when relationships break down.
Blessed are those who are involved in the arms trade,
  for theirs are the best deals in developing nations.
Blessed are the directors of privatised utilities,
  for theirs are the fat cat bonuses.

(I am indebted to those guests at Spring Harvest 1997 who provided creative possibilities for alternative Beatitudes while attending my Bible readings from the Sermon on the Mount. One group suggested a delightfully apposite mid-nineties beatitude, although I suspect its pertinence will be lost all too quickly, given the average shelf-life of today's pop icons: 'Blessed are the Spice Girls, because they get what they want, what they really, really want.')

The benefits attached to the Beatitudes sustain the general and pervasive sense of beauty and mystery. In fact the promises are even more allusive than the qualities of life affirmed by the Beatitudes. They consistently provoke two questions: *When* will the blessed be comforted, or see God? *How* is the kingdom theirs, and how will they inherit the earth?

One structural device is immediately apparent, for the first and eighth blessings are identical: 'theirs is the kingdom of heaven' (5:3, 10). In this way Jesus provides a poetical sense of completeness to his picture of the blessed state, rounding off the Beatitudes with a deliberate repetition. Inheriting the kingdom is therefore the generic description of the blessed. The intervening promises represent different facets of what it means to receive this glorious blessing from God.

The time zones indicated by the Beatitudes are typical of Jesus' teaching on the kingdom of God. A new age of blessing has commenced in space and time with the start of his public ministry, so the Great Sermon confidently proclaims that Jesus' disciples can enter and experience a 'now dimension' of blessedness. But the entirety, the fullness of Jesus' Beatitudes has not yet been made immediately available. There is a present inbreaking of the kingdom of blessedness, a partial fulfilment in the present, and this is designed to quicken in Jesus' followers a longing for the future, the perfect and complete consummation of these promises of blessedness when the kingdom comes in power at the end of the age. It is quite impossible to begin to understand Jesus' teaching without recognising the decisive place given to this partially realised eschatology, the now and not-yet dimensions held in tension. He proclaims that the age of the kingdom has already begun, and he simultaneously encourages his followers to await its completion with great expectancy, as they devote their lives to the pursuit of the virtues so persuasively commended by Jesus' glorious Beatitudes.

4

Eight Steps to Fulfilment –
the Characteristics of the Blessed
Matthew 5:3–12

The bestseller lists have been filled for years with 'how to' books. Practical steps for personal success are offered for every sphere of life from career to marriage, from stress management to dog training. The world is awash with advice, much of it unconvincing, hyped or next to useless. Two thousand years ago Jesus provided eight steps to personal fulfilment. But these steps begin from a different orientation from most of today's recommended habits for successful living. For Jesus, the key is to be more of a giver than a taker, more concerned with serving than acquiring. He introduces us to an 'upside down' mode of living that blatantly repudiates the prevailing assumptions not only of first-century Palestine, but also of Western society at the end of the second millennium. Some suggest that Christianity has had its day, and now the post-Christian world needs to experiment with alternative religions and therapies. The simple truth is that no country and lamentably few churches have ever had the courage to embrace without equivocation Jesus' radical strategy for a life that is truly blessed.

Blessed are the poor in spirit

Among the Jews, the word 'poor' had developed a double significance. First, it described the materially poor, those who were marginalised and excluded from the wealth enjoyed by the privileged and successful. Second, it indicated a response to God because in the ancient world, if Jews fell on hard times and there was no one else to turn to, they would almost inevitably and instinctively cry out to God for mercy. The Friend of the poor would become their Rescuer. On Jesus' lips, the phrase 'poor in spirit' would inevitably echo these traditions. He is not turning material poverty into a virtue, but he recognises that the materially poor can also discover a spiritual poverty which spurs them on to a closer walk with God. This does not exclude from Jesus' promise those who are better off. Irrespective of material circumstances, the same blessing is extended in equal measure upon all who discover what it means to become poor in spirit.

Despite this noble tradition of the spiritual benefits that could arise in the midst of the deprivation and destitution of material misfortune, by the time of Jesus the term 'poor' had fallen into disrepute. The social and religious élite among the Jews, the Sadducees and Herodians, the Pharisees and scribes had all come to despise the poor of the land – those Jews of low birth and nominal education, who neither knew the scriptures nor took synagogue attendance very seriously. It was not just the prostitutes and tax collectors, but the great swathe of ordinary people whom the Pharisees in particular sought to avoid. They shunned the poor for fear of spiritual contamination and they condemned them as beyond redemption. No effort need be made to bring repentance and spiritual enlightenment to such people – they were the lowest of the low.

Jesus obliterates the arrogance and complacency of religious and social élitism. He once explained that he had come for the spiritually sick because only the spiritually sick have need of a doctor (Mt 9:12). The implication is stark: those who preen their religious pedigree, taking pride in their spiritual accomplishments, exclude themselves from the place of blessing. Without poverty of spirit, there can be no entry into the promise of the first beatitude.

Spiritual poverty has two distinct dimensions: our impotence and our sinfulness. As to impotence, Zechariah had eloquently prophesied that God's great redemptive purposes upon the face of the earth were critically dependent not upon human might or power, but upon the provision of the Holy Spirit (Zech 4:6). Jesus spelled out this same principle of absolute dependence upon God with unapologetic directness: 'Apart from me you can do nothing' (Jn 15:5).

How often the pathway to a failed vision has been paved with good intentions. How often we have tried to do great things for God in our own resources, and ended up disappointed. Luke emphasised that even when Jesus set his followers a global task in the Great Commission, he expressly forbade premature attempts to launch into world mission. First they had to wait in the city until they were clothed with power from on high (Lk 24:49). Sadly the modern church has sometimes attempted to engage in decades of evangelism, months of mission and other commendable initiatives without giving sufficient expression to this fundamental and enduring dependence upon the resources of God. In order to receive the blessing due to those who are poor in spirit, we need to rediscover our spiritual impotence. We are simply and wholly unable to fulfil our potential as the servants of God until we discover our absolute dependence upon the resources of heaven. Unless we become 'poor in spirit', we will never be able to achieve anything of enduring spiritual significance.

As to the spiritual poverty of our sinfulness, Isaiah experienced this with rare intensity during his vision of the Lord's holy presence filling the temple. Here was not merely a recognition of the sinful state of the nation – 'I live among a people of unclean lips' – but also a discovery of personal sinfulness – 'I am a man of unclean lips'. The unspeakable purity of the holiness of God exposed the secrets of his own heart. Sin was no longer understood to make an intermittent appearance in his life in terms of occasional wrongdoing. Instead sin was now seen to have made its home in his heart, staining and corrupting the essential fabric of his being. Isaiah made the transition from acknowledging particular sins to discovering his own innate sinfulness. This shocking discovery explains the intensity of his heartfelt cry: 'I am ruined . . . my eyes have seen the King, the Lord Almighty' (Is 6:5).

Later in the prophecies of Isaiah this experience of a personal discovery of sinfulness is universalised as the defining and fatal flaw of the human condition: 'All of us have become like one who is unclean, and all our righteous acts are like filthy rags' (Is 64:6). The inclusiveness of the description is emphatic. 'All of us' signifies a condition without exception. In London in the heat of midsummer, few places can be as revolting as a tube train in the late afternoon rush hour, heaving with people and heavy with a working day's body odour. If cattle were herded so tightly into trucks there would be a public outrage. However, if a tramp gets onto the train, stinking of fresh beer and stale urine, at the next station everyone else will make a sudden rush for the door. The tramp alone can be guaranteed a seat on the train, scrupulously avoided by the city workers. Isaiah's assertion is extraordinary: in the eyes of God, who sees the secret sinfulness of our inner being, we are more unclean, more filthy than that tramp.

'All our righteous acts' indicates that even our best moments are inescapably tarnished. A beach with warning flags flying can be a great place to admire the majestic force of waves crashing upon the beach, but the flags alert us to hidden currents or an undertow that can suck the unsuspecting swimmer under water and out to sea. Isaiah suggests that the tragedy of the human condition, our inner contradiction, is found in the unsavoury truth that even our highest virtues are fatally flawed by the undertow of self-serving, sinful motivation.

Isaiah invites us to consider his bleak summary of the human condition not as a diagnosis of the character defects of professional criminals, nor as a mere opinion of an ancient Hebrew pessimist or misanthropist, but as a brutally frank depiction of our universal standing before God. When we enter into Isaiah's perspective, we begin to discover what it means to become 'poor in spirit'.

Only when Isaiah had expressed his cry of desolation could he experience God's forgiving mercy and receive his commission to serve as a prophet. Only when we come to a similar depth of self-awareness, facing up to our personal, innate and inescapable sinfulness, can we enter into the blessing that Jesus attached to the condition of being poor in spirit. The blessedness to which Jesus invites us therefore begins not from achieving sufficient spiritual merit, but from discovering our acute spiritual inadequacy. The General Confession sums up the foundational reality of our spiritual poverty: 'There is no health in us.'

Blessed are those who mourn

Some Christians have suggested that grief is off limits for believers, a superfluous set of emotional responses for those who live in the confident hope of resurrection from the dead. Such an approach is perverse, denying genuine emotions under a repressive cold-hearted doctrinal overstatement, as cruel as it is unreal. When Jesus stood near the tomb of his good friend Lazarus, he wept (Jn 11:35). There was no shame, no sense of failure in his weeping. Rather he demonstrated the fullness of his humanity and the naturalness of grief. The more we love, the more it hurts when loved ones are taken from us. To mourn is not to sin, but to be human.

The second beatitude has often proved a profound source of comfort to the bereaved. The words of Jesus by no means rebuke us in our mourning, but rather promise that during and beyond a season of sorrow, we can also know the comfort of God. This comfort is both future and present. Future because Jesus' resurrection from the dead gives us confidence that by faith in him we have received everlasting life. Present because we are sustained not only by this hope of life beyond the grave, but also because the love of God can support us even in the midst of our present loss.

While this promise of comfort to the bereaved is enduring, sensitive and strong, we should not restrict Jesus' meaning to the literal context of mourning in the face of death. Two other dimensions of mourning can be identified in the Bible, and these are both concerned with sorrow over sin – that of others, and our own. When Jesus looked upon Jerusalem, he not only spoke words of judgement against the hypocrisy and love of power that had almost always characterised the city, he also grieved at the lostness of her inhabitants: 'O Jerusalem, Jerusalem, you who kill the prophets and stone those sent to you, how often I have longed to gather your children together, as a hen gathers her chicks under her wings, but you were not willing. Look, your house is left to you desolate' (Mt 23:37–38).

Here is mourning for the sins of others. Jesus does not merely condemn Jerusalem, he grieves over her consistent refusal to return to the ways of God. While the disciples were captivated by the wonderful buildings of the Temple precinct, many of which had been constructed and improved by Herod the Great, Jesus was more aware of the present and imminent consequences of the spiritual barrenness of the place once known as the city of God. '"Look, Teacher!

What massive stones! What magnificent buildings!" "Do you see all these great buildings?" replied Jesus. "Not one stone here will be left on another; every one will be thrown down"' (Mk 13:1–2).

Mourning is not the same as misery. Jesus knew how to have fun, and evidently took pleasure in meals and parties. Those who had criticised John the Baptist for his strict asceticism employed the opposite accusation against Jesus, exaggerating his warm-hearted socialising into the charge that he was a glutton and a drunkard (Mt 11:19). However, while Jesus could never be called morbid or a kill-joy, he was not someone devoted to the superficial pleasures of life. His mourning over Jerusalem reveals that he never lost sight of ultimate reality and the foundational need to be right with God.

When I was writing my book on the Ten Commandments, I needed to research all manner of corruption in the life of the nation. There were times when I needed to leave my computer and go for a walk in the garden, almost overcome with a sense of sorrow at the moral degradation of the Western world and our callous disregard for the victims of a lifestyle built around looking after number one. If we are to mourn over the sin of a city or a nation, a vital distinction must be drawn between us and Jesus. In his case, there was exemption from sin. In ours, there can never be any justification for setting ourselves up in self-righteousness over against the state of the nation. Like Nehemiah, we need to confess the sins both of our nation and ourselves, identifying with our fellow sinners in their hour of need: 'When I heard these things, I sat down and wept. For some days I mourned and fasted and prayed before the God of heaven . . . "I confess the sins we Israelites, including myself and my father's house, have committed against you. We have acted very wickedly towards you"' (Neh 1:4, 6–7).

Christians have sometimes experienced this sense of

mourning at times of national celebration. When others are at their most positive, we can become the odd ones out, sensing the hidden calamity of complacent sinfulness. The year 2000 is likely to result in record numbers of hangovers when many people indulge in party-going as never before. Christians need not exempt themselves from partying (as opposed to drunkenness!), since Jesus himself was so keen on attending and enjoying social occasions. But in the midst of happiness it should not surprise us if sometimes a sense of sorrow wells up within. Even those of us who are very definitely party animals may sometimes experience a measure of detachment from the fun that surrounds us. An inescapable impulse may arise to grieve for those who are excluded from the great party of the West – usually the poor and the elderly – and to mourn for a society that knows how to party but has forgotten the ways of justice, repentance and living faith.

While Jesus' reaction to Jerusalem is the definitive example of mourning *over the sins of others*, the citizens of Jerusalem in the time of Ezra and Nehemiah experienced a spontaneous mourning *over their own sins*. Once the task of rebuilding the city walls was complete, the leaders of the nation had planned a great public celebration. As Ezra and the Levites read from the ancient Law of Moses there was an unexpected reaction. Despite the encouragement of the leaders to enjoy a day of celebration, the people were caught up in spontaneous weeping, overwhelmed by an unexpected and deep conviction of sin (Neh 8). The result of the weeping was a day of public fasting, confession and repentance: the people gathered wearing sackcloth, with ashes on their heads, confessing the sins of themselves and their fathers (Neh 9). Out of confession came a fresh start, a renewed covenant with God, which led in turn to a festival of praise that was wholehearted and exuberant. This time there was no need for the leaders of the nation to stir the people to worship, and the sound of their celebration could be heard a great distance from the city (Neh 10–12). The mourning for sin was not therefore an end in itself, but the necessary prelude to thoroughgoing, practical repentance and a moral renewal in the life of the nation.

Jonathan Edwards recorded a similar corporate experience of mourning over sin during the Great Awakening. He was preaching at a church that was known for the spiritual indifference of some of the men. Before the service they demonstrated their bored detachment by leaning casually on pillars at the back of the building. When Edwards finished preaching the men were still leaning against the pillars, but now there was no hint of detachment or boredom. Overcome by conviction of sin, the men clutched at the pillars as if the floor was about to open beneath them, allowing them to be swallowed into hell itself. It was a small step from such a profound awareness of sin and its eternal consequences to receive personal salvation through faith in Christ.

There is a crucial difference between these two kinds of mourning for sin. We can mourn over the sins of others, but we cannot repent on their behalf. However, when we mourn over our own sin, the mourning is not an end in itself but an emotional reaction to the discovery of the depths and significance of our sin. This naturally leads us on towards repentance, forgiveness and a fresh start in life.

We have tended to make too little of sin in recent years. In the secular world, guilt feelings have been treated as a psychological malfunction in need of a cure. Some obviously do suffer from irrational, misplaced and excessive guilt feelings which may well benefit from such treatment, but there still exists such a thing as *real guilt*, the objective reality of standing under the judgement of God because of our sinful living. The Bible gives us many insights into the sinfulness of sin – that is, the severity of its impact upon our lives both in the present and for all eternity. Jeremiah's prophecies diagnosed the human condition to be beyond cure, suggesting that the eradication of sin was as likely as a leopard changing its spots. He argued that we have become so accustomed to doing evil that uncontaminated good is beyond our accomplishment (Jer 13:23). The human heart, Jeremiah concluded, is deceitful above all things and beyond cure (Jer 17:9). Ezekiel spoke of a heart of stone, and the need to receive a new 'heart of flesh' from God (Ezek 11:19; 36:26). Paul gave a similar diagnosis not merely of his own heart, but of the essential crisis of the human condition: 'For I have the desire to do what is good, but I cannot carry it out. For what I do is not the good I want to do; no, the evil I do not want to do – this I keep on doing' (Rom 7:18–19). Faced with this inner contradiction between good intentions and selfish actions, Paul expressed an agony of heart: 'What a wretched man I am! Who will rescue me from this body of death?' (Rom 7:24).

This intensity of self-recrimination is nothing less than mourning for sin – not on this occasion the sin of the world, but the sinfulness of Paul's own inner life. There have been seasons in my own life when I have agonised over the depths of my own sinfulness, the selfish instincts that find expression so easily, the inability to change quickly, thoroughly and lastingly into a closer conformity with the character of Christ. The first such experience was the worst. Since no one else in my church spoke about an inner struggle with sin, I assumed that my own difficulties were unique and indicated an acute spiritual inadequacy and failure. In truth, the more clearly we see our own character – our instinctive bias to selfishness and impurity in contrast with the glorious, spontaneous and consistent self-giving love of Christ – the more likely we are to enter into an experience of mourning over sin. This mourning is not reserved for the exceptionally wicked; it can find a valid and valuable place in the spiritual experience of every believer.

To all such agony of spirit the second beatitude speaks words of comfort. The rest of the New Testament explains that this comfort is extended in three complementary ways: present forgiveness through the grace of God in Christ; once-for-all liberation beyond the grave from the sinful nature; and the abiding presence of the Holy Spirit through whom we can seek to cultivate the spiritual fruit of a character that is being renewed. If we are to experience the fullness of Jesus' promise of comfort to those who mourn, we need to rediscover what it means, as individuals and corporately, to mourn over the sin of our nation and also over our own sin.

Blessed are the meek

Of all the Beatitudes, Jesus' blessing upon the meek has caused the most derision. 'Meek' is a word hardly ever used today, but its connotations are largely negative. It brings to mind the picture of a tongue-tied and lisping schoolchild, shy and nervous on their first day at school. Meekness seems a childish form of weakness. While self-help sections in bookshops offer an increasing number of titles on assertiveness training for everyone from the bullied child to the person overlooked for promotion, no one today is in a hurry to learn about meekness. So is the third beatitude anything other than an embarrassment for adult Christians facing the harsh, competitive realities of the modern world?

Swinburne, a lyrical and dissolute late-Romantic poet of the Victorian era, saw nothing virtuous in meekness. He lamented the dominance of Christianity in the West as the triumph of the 'pale Galilean'. Nietzsche was the philosophical champion of late-nineteenth-century opposition to Jesus. For Nietzsche, the greatest of virtues was the will to power:

> What is good? – All that heightens the feeling of power, the will to power, power itself in man.
> What is bad? – All that proceeds from weakness.
> What is happiness? – The feeling that power *increases* – that resistance is overcome . . .
>
> (Nietzsche, *The Anti-Christ*, 2)

Nietzsche therefore denounced what he considered the sheer folly and weakness of Jesus' emphasis on compassion and kindness.

> The great men of antique morality, Epictetus for example, knew nothing of the now normal glorification of thinking of others, of living for others; in the light of our moral fashion they would have to be called downright immoral, for they strove with all their might *for* their *ego* and *against* feeling with others (that is to say, with the sufferings and moral frailties of others). Perhaps they would reply to us: 'If you are so boring or ugly an object to yourself, by all means think of others more than of yourself! It is right you should!' (Nietzsche, *Daybreak*, 131)

Nietzsche was confident that the only way for the Western world to break free from prevailing weakness and enter the age of the superman was to repudiate the enervating anti-power influence of Jesus – 'out of fear the reverse type has been willed, bred, achieved: the domestic animal, the herd animal, the sick animal man – the Christian' (Nietzsche, *The Anti-Christ*, 3–4). Nietzsche's natural successor in the political arena, who appropriated and applied his anti-Christian values more rigorously than anyone else has ever dared, was of course Adolf Hitler.

When John Wesley preached on the Beatitudes he insisted that meekness should not be confused with apathy. Towards God, meekness means humble obedience. Towards others, meekness prompts us to be gentle and humble, sensitive and patient. Meekness therefore requires a willingness to accept the role of servant. Meekness leaves no place for pushiness, self-vindication and the stubbornness that refuses to give any ground.

The British have traditionally had an almost insatiable appetite for dressing up in public: members of the House of Lords, lawyers in court and senior clergy all make a public display of their social status by wearing archaic costumes. In the eighties 'power dressing' entered our vocabulary to signify clothes designed to make an imposing impression in the workplace. In a status-sensitive world, people become acutely aware of how others treat them. Access to the senior staff dining room, a key to the director's private toilet, a place in the car park reserved in your name – many build their sense of self-worth upon their perks, prestige and promotion prospects. Some people put on airs, expecting special, even reverential treatment from office juniors, secretaries or supermarket cashiers. We are trained in the simple equation that to push ourselves forward, we need to put others down.

In Jewish history, Israel was delivered from Egypt and later from Babylon not in strength, but in weakness. Their battles belonged to the Lord (e.g. 1 Sam 17:47). Similarly in Christian history, the most significant advances of the church have been in weakness. When the church has attempted to use methods of self-assertion, the result has been tragedy: the wretched and shameful history of the Crusades, the Spanish Inquisition, and the drowning of those who practised believers' baptism by both Catholics and Magisterial Protestants at the time of the Reformation.

Paul gave the Philippians advice that parallels Jesus' commendation of meekness: 'Let your gentleness be evident to all' (Phil 4:5). He offered this practical wisdom from prison, evidently passing on to his fellow Christians an approach he had adopted himself. Each day he was chained to members of the Palace Guard, who presumably were not reluctant to treat him roughly. It is also possible that the experience extended Paul's vocabulary as he endured the soldiers' constant and casual cursing.

Faced with such restrictions on his personal privacy, Paul may have been tempted to assert himself, declaring that those who treated him badly would pay for it in the eternal suffering of hell. But Paul was not a man to give in easily to natural human instincts without meditating first upon the example of Christ. In Jesus' own captivity, no word of aggression passed his lips. He not only refused to attack the officials who organised his mock trials and the soldiers who tortured him, he also declined to use any words of self-vindication. This was in direct fulfilment of Isaiah's prophecy of the suffering servant's response to his assailants: 'He was oppressed and afflicted, yet he did not open his mouth; he was led like a lamb to the slaughter, and as a sheep before her shearers is silent, so he did not open his mouth' (Is 53:7).

Paul's advice extends the practice of meekness and gentleness into every aspect of life. Whenever our status or power allows us to dominate others, the example of Christ calls us instead to the meekness of service. Domination and assertiveness can be physical or verbal, but meekness calls us to renounce our ability to control, bully or dictate to others.

Meekness is not a way out for wimps. Meekness is when the strong choose to serve others rather than control them. When Jesus was arrested he insisted that his disciples put away their swords. Even though he could have called upon an angelic cavalry to come to his aid, the purposes of God were best fulfilled by servanthood: 'The Son of Man did not come to be served, but to serve, and to give his life as a ransom for many' (Mt 20:28).

The meek do not expect or demand special treatment. They are not easily slighted and do not quickly take offence.

Rather than expecting to be treated with special favour, the meek experience genuine surprise whenever they become the centre of attention. Meekness is the enemy of pride and disqualifies us from the lust for status and deferential treatment. Since meekness is the way of blessedness, too many of us expend far too much energy and emotion in a futile quest for the bogus blessing of public recognition, whether at work or in church. Meekness, in short, obliges us to stop taking ourselves too seriously.

The great concern of the meek is not whether they are receiving sufficient respect, but rather whether others are receiving their due. The meek will be considerate and attentive to shop assistants and waiters. The meek will be grateful if a secretary makes them a cup of coffee, rather than taking such attention for granted. The meek may even take a turn making the coffee themselves. When I was a student in Oxford, I deeply regretted the way many students treated those who served them. I longed to see the members of the Senior Common Room serve Christmas dinner to the kitchen staff in order to correct the callow arrogance of some young undergraduates.

Once, after I had been teaching on meekness and gentleness, a senior businessman confided in me that this gospel principle had cut him to the quick. Harold had always been a man of great integrity at work, never speaking a dishonest word, fixing a crooked deal, or fiddling his expenses. But when it came to personal relationships he was an absolute bully, tyrannising his underlings and treating them with casual disdain. As he reflected on his attitudes, he recognised that his underlying motivation was insecurity: fearful that his junior colleagues might knock him off his perch, he protected his own back through domineering forcefulness. He wanted to make sure that those he feared had even greater reason to be afraid of him. However explicable psychologically, such an attitude to colleagues is entirely unacceptable for the Christian. The witness of his integrity was entirely devalued by his dictatorial and dehumanising management style. He realised that the meekness and gentleness of Christ required a complete and radical overhaul in the way he wielded authority and exercised leadership.

Meekness is not rooted in weakness, but in toughness. It takes strength to serve. We need courage to lay down our pride, treat everyone we meet with dignity, and refuse to take ourselves too seriously. It was meekness that prompted Jesus to wash his disciples' feet (Jn 13:5). It is meekness that will restore a servant heart to the church.

Blessed are those who hunger and thirst for righteousness

Many of us are more than willing to eat a chocolate bar if it is put before us, but we lack the consuming passion of a true chocaholic. For those dedicated to the delights of the cocoa bean, the craving for a fresh intake of chocolate needs to be satisfied at regular intervals. In the fourth beatitude, Jesus is not commending a vague and general preference for goodness, but rather a central, pivotal, consuming and urgent priority.

In American elections, every candidate is guaranteed to be in favour of motherhood and apple pie. Similarly, for the ancient Jews, everyone would be notionally in favour of God's righteousness finding expression in the ways of the nation. Jesus expressly uses the language of appetite to describe a much more emphatic concern. To 'hunger and thirst' after righteousness means that God's ways become our meat and drink. Jesus' words indicate an ardent desire, a compelling motivation, a life focus on this priority that puts everything else into second place.

'Righteousness' is multi-layered in the Bible. On the one hand it speaks of personal holiness. The way of personal salvation requires a measure of urgency – we have to understand our need of Christ and his death for us. We also need to grasp something of the double passion of God: for the sake of his own righteousness, he was unable simply to ignore our sin and leave it unpunished; but because of his mercy towards men and women, he was not prepared to abandon us to the eternal consequences of our disastrous spiritual and moral rebellion (Rom 3:21–26). We find righteousness by faith in Christ, because we receive forgiveness and his right standing before the Father. But we also need to continue to seek after personal righteousness in two ways: inner life change, so that more of Christ's character might be formed within us; and a closer walk with God, in whom righteousness finds full expression. There is therefore a present and future fulfilment of Jesus' promise that we will be 'filled', that our spiritual appetite will be satisfied. In the present, by conversion we are already in Christ and secure in his righteousness. In heaven our encounter with God will be complete and our sinful nature will be stripped away completely.

Although these dimensions of personal salvation and a continuing quest for growth in holiness are glorious gospel truths, on their own they still represent a truncated gospel. It is impossible to study the Old Testament without recognising that the language of 'righteousness' applies to the ordering of society as well as to personal holiness. Isaiah denounced Israel for pursuing religious correctness while ignoring the exploitation of the poor: 'Yet on the day of your fasting, you do as you please and exploit all your workers' (Is 58:3).

God's preferred fast is a fasting from injustice; for those with money, influence and power to pursue righteousness in delivering a new deal for the oppressed, the workers and the refugees: 'Is not this the kind of fasting I have chosen: to loose the chains of injustice and untie the cords of the yoke, to set the oppressed free and break every yoke? Is it not to share your food with the hungry and to provide the poor wanderer with shelter . . . ?' (Is 58:6–7). The connection with righteousness is absolutely explicit: 'Then your light will break forth like the dawn, and your healing will quickly appear; then your righteousness will go before you, and the glory of the Lord will be your rear guard' (Is 58:8).

The same connection is pursued by Amos with an even greater bluntness: 'I hate, I despise your religious feasts; I cannot stand your assemblies . . . Away with the noise of your songs! I will not listen to the music of your harps. But let justice roll on like a river, righteousness like a never-failing stream!' (Amos 5:21, 23–24).

When Jesus speaks of an abiding appetite for 'righteousness', the implications for his original Jewish audience would inevitably include this societal dimension that resounded so vigorously in the words of their prophets. The Old Testament is certainly not sweepingly dismissive of financial good sense and the profit motive, but it does insist that commercial enterprise has to be set in a larger context of righteousness in which the rich can never be justified in turning a blind eye to the living conditions of the poor.

In the modern world, the Christian capitalist who pursues personal holiness while ripping off his workers is entirely in error if he thinks he is fulfilling the fourth beatitude. Without a different attitude in the workplace, he stands under the condemnation of Isaiah and Amos. So long as his employees are exploited, his bills are paid late and his Third World suppliers are locked into unjust contracts, his worship, prayer and tithing are worthless. Some right wing Christians have been so opposed to Marxism they have become blind to the social implications of the gospel. Long before Marx, and far from the destructive excesses of twentieth-century communism, the Old Testament prophets established beyond contradiction that God's righteous purposes for human society set a very high priority upon justice for the poor.

To hunger and thirst indicates a continuing appetite for righteousness. We are called to stand up for the poor and the unemployed, the elderly and the disabled, ethnic minorities and refugees, and babies in the womb under threat of abortion on demand. Similarly we must take an unyielding stand against racism and sexism, sleaze and corruption, the destruction of the environment, and the pillaging of the developing nations – not least through punitive interest rates from the World Bank and the International Monetary Fund that have led to a disguised form of economic enslavement to the West.

All too often the churches' prescriptions for society have proved naive and simplistic. The cynic is a disappointed idealist, and short-term naivete can quickly mutate into entrenched and lifelong cynicism, dismissive of all political initiatives as merely self-serving schemes that may win votes but will never make a significant practical difference. Despite every evidence of intractable injustice, both within a nation and between the developed and developing world, the Christian is called to refuse the temptations of despair or indifference. We need to cultivate a resolute and determined appetite for righteousness in business and politics, as well as in our personal lives.

Biblical righteousness is far more than a political programme or a code of conduct for personal holiness. The concept finds glorious embodiment in the character of Christ. To seek righteousness in its fullest sense means walking close to God, reading the book of righteousness, pursuing the life of righteousness, and keeping in step with the Spirit of righteousness. The fourth beatitude calls us to nothing less than whole-life discipleship: the pietist gospel is incomplete if it ignores the social dimensions of righteousness; the social justice gospel is equally incomplete if it ignores the necessity of personal salvation and the importance of personal spirituality and holiness. In every aspect of life Jesus invites us to aspire to an increasing expression of the righteousness of God.

There is an implicit danger attached to the fourth beatitude, for when we lose this hunger and thirst we are in trouble. Such loss of appetite for righteousness may arise through weariness or disappointment, through cynicism or complacency, through distraction or loss of zeal. Whenever our appetite is weak, we need to confess our indifference and pray for a fresh quickening. Above all we need to remember that the priority of righteousness is not impersonal or abstract. In Isaiah's wonderful poem of invitation, he echoes the familiar words of Middle Eastern water carriers and street vendors, but spiritual food and drink are available without charge to the faithful. The one who satisfies this hunger and thirst and then stirs us to pursue an ever increasing expression of his righteousness, as individuals and in society, is none other than the God of righteousness himself.

> Come, all you who are thirsty,
>   come to the waters;
> and you who have no money,
>   come, buy and eat!
> Come, buy wine and milk
>   without money and without cost.
> Why spend money on what is not bread,
>   and your labour on what does not satisfy?
> Listen, listen to me, and eat what is good,
>   and your soul will delight in the richest of fare.
>
>   (Is 55:1–2)

Blessed are the merciful "Krenye"

A policeman once told me of a convicted criminal who waited twenty-five years for pay back time. Through a quarter of a century he was burning with hatred, consumed with the need to do to others what they had done to him. His whole life was built around the pursuit of revenge. Sadly this is not an exceptional case. Some seek revenge through violence, some through back-stabbing in the boardroom. In some families, revenge is not fulfilled until the reading of a will, when a cats' home receives more money than the relative who had been despised by the deceased.

Shakespeare's *Hamlet* is the most famous example of a type of play known as a revenge tragedy. These were extremely popular in the last years of the sixteenth century and the first decade of the seventeenth. Private revenge was condemned in English law on two counts: it failed to accept the vengeful prerogative of God as Supreme Judge ('"Vengeance is mine," says the Lord') and at the same time it would produce anarchy by usurping the powers of the state and the sovereign to impose punishment upon the guilty through due process of law. Nonetheless, according to the customs of the day, three circumstances made private revenge acceptable, even honourable. First, where injury had resulted from treachery, revenge through deceit was legitimate. Second, revenge was sanctioned where a wrong had been done but the absence of witnesses or a loophole in the law meant that there was no legal redress. Third, and above all, many thought that private revenge was entirely justified as a result of murder, which was recognised as the ultimate crime. It was even suggested that there was a duty of revenge and that without exacting revenge a son had no honourable right to inherit his murdered father's property or name. The avenger was therefore seen to be a man of courage and honour, fulfilling a duty to his family by requiring a life for a life. The revenge tragedies pursue this legitimisation of private revenge to its logical conclusion: in their last scenes, the stage usually becomes littered with corpses as the various quests for revenge reach their bloody fulfilment.

The quest for revenge has cast long shadows from the last days of the British Empire. After the Easter uprising in Dublin in 1916, the British army decided to execute the leaders of the rebellion. Far from eliminating the republican movement, this ruthlessness only served to stir up a general revulsion against British rule. The aftershocks still resound in Northern Ireland, where the people have long tribal memories. Neither Unionists nor Republicans show much inclination to bury the hatchet, forget the past and renounce all quest for revenge in order to pursue a just and lasting peace settlement. Intransigence and bitterness, hostility and a fork-tongued double-talk still seem to be the prevailing attitudes.

Similarly in Amritsar, India, during the last days of the Empire the British troops opened fire – this time on an unarmed crowd. The casual and inhumane ruthlessness of the British was appalling, treating with absolute contempt those who presumed to resist the inalienable right of the British to rule the world. Once again the vengeful, imperial brutality completely backfired, provoking not compliance and surrender but a deepening resistance to British rule. During 1997, when Queen Elizabeth II visited India to take part in the celebrations of fifty years of independence, it was plain that many had not forgotten these acts of barbarism. Some demanded an apology, which seemed perfectly reasonable. Others demanded nothing less than revenge against 'a queen with blood on her hands'.

One of the most astonishing and unforgettable images of recent years was Nelson Mandela's release from prison in South Africa. After spending a devastating proportion of his adult life behind bars, it would have been understandable to hear from him a passionate cry for revenge. But Mandela's eye was on a higher priority: the rebirth of his nation as a 'one person, one vote' democracy. His repudiation of revenge was a remarkable act of statesmanship. While revenge is the instinctive human response, mercy makes better political sense.

The implications of Jesus' call for mercy reach far wider than acts of revenge. In school exams, on the playing fields and in management training, many are trained in the virtues of being competitive, to which there can surely be no reasonable objection. But there is such a thing as being over-competitive. At some schools, games teachers now teach the first team how to perform and conceal 'professional fouls'. In some businesses, sales reps are expected to engage in sharp practices against their competitors. In politics, it sometimes seems that the first conditions of advancement are a willingness to be 'economical with the truth' and a preparedness to stab opponents and colleagues in the back.

A lack of mercy is not merely vengeful, but shows a disregard or even contempt for the human dignity of victims, readily taking advantage of others and kicking them when they are down. In September 1997 a study by researchers at the University of Leeds explored the values of young professionals, the successors to the yuppies of the eighties. Representing 27 per cent of society, two-thirds of these ambitious and wealthy people thought they had no responsibility at all to help those worse off than themselves (*The Times*, Friday 5 September 1997).

Turning to Jesus, his life was consistently marked by the priority of being merciful. He was patient and compassionate to the many who brought the sick and demonised for him to heal. He looked upon the masses as 'sheep without a shepherd' (Mt 9:36) and so devoted much time to teaching them about the kingdom of God and how it could become a living reality in their lives. Faced with the woman caught in adultery, Jesus refused simply to condemn her, urging instead a fresh start in life in response to his offer of forgiveness (Jn 8:3–11). In his teaching, Jesus commended the Good Samaritan, who did not merely give to charity but was prepared to put himself out, making time for the inconveniently needy (Lk 10:30–37). Even on the cross, Jesus persisted with his commitment to mercy, praying that God would forgive those who had strung him up to die (Lk 23:34).

The early church embraced the priority of mercy, not merely in seeking to forgive their persecutors, but in reaching out with compassion to the marginalised. While others turned a blind eye to the poor, the disciples of Christ had no excuse. In the New Testament there is a consistent emphasis upon practical mercy towards the poor and widows within the church (see Acts 6:1; 1 Tim 5:3). In the fourth century, an official report to the Emperor Julian was indignant at the extent of the Christians' initiatives of mercy: 'The impious Galileans support not merely their own poor but ours as well.'

At its best the church has continued this great tradition of mercy. Christian initiatives can be seen in the founding of hospitals and hospices, in establishing schools for those who are unable to pay for the privilege, in campaigning for the abolition of slavery, and in the provision of aid and development initiatives for the Two-Thirds World. Of course there is always more that could be done and Christians are by no means the only people to show mercy, but research into charitable giving has consistently shown that Christian faith tends to make individuals become more generous.

In the modern Western world two key trends combine to make mercy an increasingly endangered virtue. On the one hand, the population is aging. In a few years' time, the dependent population will exceed the working population. Already hospital and residential care for the elderly is being marginalised, as younger generations prove increasingly reluctant to accept the necessary tax burden. At the same time, the power of materialism dictates that money and possessions matter more than anything else in life. This means that society is showing a tendency to become increasingly selfish, wanting levels of taxation to be continually reduced. As a result, states across the West show signs of steadily withdrawing from responsibility to care for the poor, the elderly, overseas aid and the support of refugees. If the church cannot persuade the state to take responsibility, the church must show mercy direct. This needs to be done not only through international aid and development charities like Tear Fund and Christian Aid, but also through local care initiatives, working alongside such charities as Shaftesbury, UK Action and Spurgeon's Child Care.

What is true for the poor should also be true for prisoners. There is a moral crisis in the West, with a rising tide of violent crime and signs that some youngsters no longer have a clear understanding of right and wrong. With a shortage of money in the coffers of the state, increasing competition for those limited financial resources from growing social needs, and an increasing number of young men and women being imprisoned, the result is increasing degradation within the prison service. In September 1997, an official report into one British prison stated that the conditions for inmates were so appalling that many would find it hard to believe that such degradation could be found in Britain at the end of the twentieth century. Mercy does not mean rejecting the notion of punishment, but it does require us to uphold the human dignity even of those who have committed appalling crimes. A dehumanising environment is almost guaranteed to prove counter-productive for any serious attempt to reform prisoners, failing to encourage them to treat others with greater respect and to repudiate the attitudes that led to a life of crime.

The fifth beatitude calls the disciples of Jesus to embrace a consistent and inclusive attitude of mercy towards those who have injured us personally, towards competitors, towards the poor and criminals in society, and even towards the enemies of our nation. Our capacity to show mercy is grounded in the cross of Christ. In the crucifixion we see a God of mercy who has responded to his enemies with extreme mercy. If we respond to others with even a small fraction of the mercy that Christ has shown to us, we are sure to develop a reputation for being merciful. Revenge and self-assertion may be the more instinctive human responses, but those who have discovered God's mercy at the cross need to explore how to express mercy in every aspect of life.

Blessed are the pure in heart

The Oscar ceremony in Hollywood is an annual celebration of many arts: acting and cinematography, fashion and plastic surgery. This is the ultimate parade of the beautiful people, where outward impression is all. Some are beautiful by birth. Others disguise less perfect features with the finest clothing, hairstyling and cosmetics. But natural good looks on the silver screen are rumoured to have become an endangered species, with ever increasing numbers seeking to augment their beauty under the surgeon's knife.

Multiple marriages, implants and liposuction, personal shrinks and fitness trainers, even personal shoppers – where Hollywood leads, the rest of the West tends to follow. Those who analyse social trends conclude that post-modernism has focused the sense of self on external image. Just as Madonna reinvented herself several times in the eighties, many ordinary people now go shopping for a 'new image', strengthening their sense of self-worth with a new dress or coat. The superficiality of this world is summed up in a standard phrase of greeting: 'Darling, you're looking wonderful!' The flattery is, of course, obligatory, irrespective of how anyone really looks at the time.

Among the Jews in the time of Jesus, those who pursued purity with most zeal were the Pharisees. Not for them a pure but cosmetic beauty, no more than skin deep. The Pharisees looked for purity of lifestyle. Their standard method, however, concentrated not on inner attitudes of heart but the external purity of religious ceremony and legalistic conformity. Faced with their criticism of his disciples' less scrupulous eating habits (they were eating in the manner of Galilean fishermen, without washing their hands first), Jesus responded with a vigorous repudiation of the effectiveness of Pharisaical fussiness:

> 'Are you so dull?' he asked. 'Don't you see that nothing that enters a man from the outside can make him "unclean"? For it doesn't go into his heart but into his stomach, and then out of his body.' (In saying this, Jesus declared all foods 'clean'.)
>
> He went on: 'What comes out of a man is what makes him "unclean". For from within, out of men's hearts, come evil thoughts, sexual immorality, theft, murder, adultery, greed, malice, deceit, lewdness, envy, slander, arrogance and folly. All these evils come from inside and make a man "unclean".' (Mk 7:18–23)

Jesus' analysis demonstrated that the external obsessions of the Pharisees were completely futile. Purity of food intake made no difference whatsoever to purity of heart. No matter how zealous the Pharisees might be, even if they attained absolute external purity their legalistic negativity would still be impotent before the ingrained impurity of the human heart.

It's not just for the Pharisees that Jesus' teaching raises acute problems. To be sure, for those who love their food it will come as some relief to discover that there is no direct connection between inner purity and dietary laws! But Jesus rejects all superficial solutions to the fundamental question: How can we ever achieve the purity of heart that Jesus commends in the sixth beatitude?

Before we pursue that question, we need to recognise the implications of this inner purity. According to Jesus' own critique, the Pharisees were like whitewashed tombs – impressive on the outside but inwardly as wholesome as a decaying corpse. The purity that Jesus commends begins in our inner being. His concept of purity is not narrowly religious, but embraces every aspect of life. Jesus rejects not only the more extreme sins that would receive almost universal opprobrium, like theft, murder and adultery, but he also has zero tolerance for more socially acceptable attitudes, like greed and envy, slander and arrogance. This purity requires not merely an abstinence from sin, but a consistent and determined cultivation of the character of Christ. Inner purity is therefore defined by the love commands: loving God with our whole being, loving our neighbour as ourselves, and loving fellow believers as Jesus has loved us.

Like Jesus himself, we are called to be open, sincere and real in all our relationships and dealings, with no masks or hidden agendas, no deceit or pretence. Computer software often claims to be WYSIWYG – what you see (on the screen) is what you get (in print). In practice it would be more precise to say that what you see is more or less what you hope to get, if your printer is having a good day. But purity of heart produces people who become reliably WYSIWYG. Purity of heart makes for genuine disciples who ring true in every situation.

How can we begin to attain the purity of heart that will fundamentally shape our relationship with God and with others?

1. *In the repentance to which Jesus called his first hearers,* we reject the instinctive sinfulness that is found in our inner

being. That is, we recognise our own 'heart of stone', in Ezekiel's phrase, and seek a new heart, softened by the purity and love of God.

2. *By faith in the risen Christ*, we accept his death on the cross not as an accident, but as God's atoning sacrifice for the lost, and through Christ we enter a new standing before the Father, 'clothed', in Wesley's glorious phrase, 'in righteousness divine'.

3. *In cultivating the fruit of the Spirit*, we set ourselves the priority not merely of outward conformity but of inner character change, growing into the wholesomeness of Christ. Character is the produce of a lifetime, so purity of heart is not a starting point but rather the mountainous heights which beckon us onwards to a lifetime of continuing ascent.

4. *By keeping short accounts with the Father*, we resist the constant inclination to surrender again to the enticements of sinfulness. Our heart has an endemic tendency to return again to stone; we quite literally have an inner bias to 'hardening of the heart'. The more frequently and readily we walk the way of repentance and renewed submission to the love of Christ, the less opportunity we give for inner impurities to take hold and destroy whatever measure of purity we have so far been able to attain.

Jesus promises a very distinct blessing for the pure in heart: they will see God. As ever, the promise is both future and present. Future, because the God of perfect holiness and purity will not inflict his eternal presence upon those who have rejected inner purity in this life. Present, because Jesus is nothing less than the Son of God incarnate, the definitive revelation of God's purity in human form. The more we seek purity, the more we recognise the unsullied inner purity of Jesus Christ. In him we are able to see God now, and as we accept and pursue his call to purity of heart, by faith in him we can experience progressive inner renewal. Through the indwelling influence of the Holy Spirit, Christ's great purpose really is to 'fit us for heaven' to live with him there.

Blessed are the peacemakers

Jesus commends not simply those who live in peace, but those who actively work to establish peace. This is the much harder path to travel. To withdraw into a cosy peace, untroubled by external pressures may sound gloriously attractive – an escape into an other-worldly safe haven. Sometimes the church has been accused of exactly this kind of other-worldliness, of being oblivious to the pressures and demands of the real world; an opiate if not for the masses, in Marx's memorable phrase, then certainly for the middle classes.

The way of Jesus is the way of peacemaking, for his entire life was built around restoring right relationships between men, women and God. Paul summed up eloquently the pivotal significance of reconciliation in the cross and the good news: 'God was reconciling the world to himself in Christ, not counting men's sins against them. And he has committed to us the message of reconciliation ... We implore you on Christ's behalf: Be reconciled to God' (2 Cor 5:19–20).

Jesus never showed any desire to pursue a tranquil and serene life as a detached mystic, living far out in the desert and inviting others to withdraw into a similarly isolated spirituality. His peacemaking responsibilities made him a determined activist throughout the three years of his public ministry, which he described as coming to 'seek and save' the lost (Lk 19:10). Above all, the iron resolve of his peacemaking is demonstrated during his final journey towards Jerusalem, where he knew he faced an agonising death, not merely because he would be rejected by men, but because he was to become as the suffering servant the necessary redemptive sacrifice. 'The Son of Man did not come to be served, but to serve, and to give his life as a ransom for many' (Mt 20:28).

Because of all that the Prince of peace has accomplished for us, we have not only been able to enter into a restored peace with God, but we are also, as Paul understood so clearly, called and enabled to pursue a similar task of peace-making and reconciliation. Our entire approach to life, at work and at home, at leisure and at church, should be informed by the peacemaking priority. We are called not merely to enjoy peace but to help others enter into the way of peace that Christ provides.

The implications of the call to be peacemakers connect with every part of life. Christians have a responsibility to provide mediation between hostile parties, whether at work, at home or in politics. We need Christians willing to take the risk of being honest brokers, bringing together intransigent opponents. I am full of admiration for those evangelicals in Northern Ireland who have worked tirelessly behind the scenes to seek to establish communication and mutual understanding between Republicans and Unionists, between democratically elected politicians and leaders of the various terrorist organisations.

Within the local church, counselling and training provision needs to enable people to understand how to work for peace and reconciliation whenever possible, in their marriages, friendships and business dealings. Whole-life discipleship requires us to provide and develop strategies that enable Christians to escape from destructive patterns in their own relationships and then to help others to explore more fully the ways of peace. Three of the crying needs of our society are connected with peacemaking: help for couples to sustain their marriages; help for parents to cope wisely with the demands of children at different stages of their development;

and help for children to cope wisely with the demands of parents, whether the children are teenagers or mature adults attending to the needs of elderly parents in declining health. Close relationships have always been capable of turning sour – most murders occur within the family! But the pressures of modern living seem to have made these relationships more fragile than ever before. A peacemaking church has the potential to become a centre of mediation and reconciliation for the local community, providing training courses shaped by biblical wisdom, and also a counselling service from which many in our society could benefit greatly.

If we take peacemaking seriously, it will also involve us in campaigning for peace, never by violent means, but always with the weapons of peace. The scandal of the vast number of abortions now taking place requires a persuasive campaign of resistance. In 1967, at the time the Abortion Act was passed, it was argued that abortion should be legalised for exceptional and difficult cases, but now abortion has become so normative that some clinics are advertising the advantages of 'an abortion in your lunch hour'. Although many would reluctantly accept that there are circumstances in which abortion is the lesser evil, 600 abortions a day in Britain surely indicates a callous and casual disregard for the sanctity of life. The most dangerous place for a baby in the West today is within its mother's womb.

At the same time, peacemakers will take a stand against the scandal of the international arms trade which plunders the national coffers of many developing nations. Peacemakers will denounce the appalling carnage of land-mines and the unspeakable horrors of nuclear, biological and chemical weapons, pressing always for international agreements that prohibit their use and destroy existing stockpiles.

Peacemakers will also ask searching questions about the wanton violence, often in lingering close up, that scars our imaginations through an increasing number of TV programmes and movies. Nor is the toy shop exempt from the peacemaker's gaze. It is one thing to zap aliens, but the peacemaker will speak out against the trend to glorify violence through video games in which the enemy is human and their death is celebrated in a digital orgy of bloodletting. Replica guns also beg questions for the peacemaker. Children instinctively play shooting games, but it is adults who blur the line between play and reality. Water pistols and space guns may be harmless enough, but do we really want children having fun with exact replicas of the semi-automatic weapons that plague our city streets after dark? Westerners are typically appalled when they see young children fighting in the front line in Third World conflicts, and then they give their own children plastic replicas of the same guns for Christmas.

Peacemaking also has ecological implications. God created a world of harmony and beauty in which every creature had its place. We have polluted the planet, devoured its non-renewable resources, devastated the rain forests, reduced fish stocks in some seas to the brink of extinction, and are clogging both the streets and our lungs with the consequences of our voracious appetite for private cars. The whole eco-system has become our prey. Insatiable consumption, without a thought for future generations, has placed the entire planet at risk. Despite all the evidence of global warming, the holes in the ozone layer and the exponential increases in carbon dioxide emissions, we have still failed to secure international agreements to stem the destructive tide – not least because the United States and China have led the way in a profoundly selfish disregard for the well-being of the planet and the inheritance we will leave to future generations. Peacemaking calls us to pray and campaign for the restoration of harmony in the eco-system, because harmony and beauty were the Creator's original intentions.

Above all, of course, peacemaking has evangelistic impli-cations. The good news of the gospel is that we can have peace with God through the death and resurrection of Christ. He has paid the price of reconciliation and opened the way for us to be right with God. If creative and persua-sive proclamation of the gospel is not central to our local church life, if we do not embrace the need for every member witness, then we have no right to be called peacemakers at all. The greatest privilege of peacemaking is surely to assist another as they make the decisive step of faith in Christ and receive the glorious gift of peace with God.

There is no promise in the Sermon on the Mount that peacemaking will be easy, always appreciated or successful. Jesus was the greatest peacemaker this world has ever known, and the thanks he received was state execution by crucifixion. In our own century, Anwar Sadat took a coura-geous initiative in seeking peace with Israel and received an Arab assassin's bullet, just as Yitzhak Rabin met a similar fate at the hands of a fellow Jew when he was making great efforts to push forward the Arab-Israeli peace process. Mar-tin Luther King devoted his life to working for civil rights for Afro-Caribbeans in the United States, resolutely empha-sising the importance of non-violent protest. He worked for a just reconciliation between the races using only the weap-ons of a man of peace. He too was assassinated. An unavoid-able risk of peacemaking is that the divided parties may both turn against the peacemaker. This is true not only in inter-national negotiations, but also in more local disputes: man-agement and union may both dismiss the approaches of the arbitration service; husband and wife may both reject the marriage counsellor's assistance. One of the ironies of Jesus' ministry is that it brought a reconciliation between two Jewish parties who were old enemies. The Herodians were wedded to Greek culture and wanted to adapt Jewish ways as much as possible to conform with the prevailing values of

Roman civilisation, while the Pharisees were committed to cultural purity, suspicious of any accommodation with Rome. Such was their common hatred for Jesus that they temporarily set aside their deep mutual antipathy, making common cause against the Prince of peace (Mk 3:6).

We are by no means called to secure peace at any price. Neville Chamberlain came back to Britain from meeting Adolf Hitler with the promise of 'peace in our time'. But the words were worthless faced with the tyrannous resolve of the Nazi leader. In the time of Jeremiah, the prophets whom the people of Israel loved to hear were those whose theme was 'Peace, peace'. Jeremiah's firm retort was that it might sound promising, but the reality of the nation's circumstances was a complete absence of peace (Jer 6:14; 8:11). The only peace that is worth pursuing, the only genuine peace, is grounded in truth, not in patching up a compromise based upon empty hopes, wishful thinking and self-deception.

While we are certainly not called to peace at any price, this gives us no excuse to become sectarian and divisive. The call to peacemaking obliges us to build bridges and to make common cause with fellow Christians in other traditions. The sad truth is that just as the most devout Jews were often violently opposed to Jesus, within the church we have often seen the destructive power of human forms of religion that have no desire to embrace and develop the virtues of peace-making. People become entrenched, embittered or over-dogmatic about secondary issues; some even make a name for themselves with a ministry based entirely on negativity, denouncing almost every other leader. I once heard about a man who was so definite about every last detail of his convictions that one by one he wrote off every church in town, until eventually he founded his own church – for himself and his family – because no one else was 'completely sound'.

The excesses of Christian disputation, the inaccuracy and misrepresentation, the simple failure even to check facts before making statements, these have frequently made the church a gross caricature of Jesus' intended community of peacemakers – more McCarthyite than Christ-like. There are indeed principles to die for – the foundational truths of the gospel that are beyond dispute or dilution. But there are also many strong opinions not worth dying for – secondary convictions that may be important but are insufficient grounds to break fellowship. Those who abandon gospel truth for the sake of peace and those who abandon gospel peacemaking for the defence of truth are in equal error, failing to understand the essential nature and interconnectedness of gospel peacemaking and gospel truth. When we have no choice but to disagree with fellow believers, we need to learn to do so as agreeably as we can, holding fast to the abiding priorities of a peacemaker.

One of the privileges of my ministry has been to sit on the Council of Management of the Evangelical Alliance. Here are baptisers of infants and baptisers of believers, representatives of the state church, historic free churches, pentecostals and new churches, Calvinists and Arminians, charismatics and non-charismatics, but all are one in Christ Jesus. On occasions when the debate has been delicate, or even potentially divisive, we have benefited immensely from those with genuine peacemaking skills – not the 'lowest common denominator' blandness that agrees so little that no progress can ever be made, but an incisive new perspective that shifts the ground of the debate. Genuine peacemaking can elevate debate to a more profound level of unity and agreement, where the differences between us fall into the shadows before the brilliance and glory of the convictions we share, the truth we defend, the Master we serve and the church we must love.

Peace with God requires repentance and faith, which in turn require an acceptance that we are sinners who need to repent and that God has the right to impose moral standards and final judgement upon rational beings within his creation. There is an offence in the gospel, both in this call to repentance and also in the scandal of the cross, which Paul recognised was objectionable both to the Jews, who demanded power not weakness, and to the Greeks, who demanded wise philosophy not an atoning sacrifice (1 Cor 1:22–23). Jesus described his own ministry as bringing a sword. Not the sword of compulsory conversion, wielded in Latin America by the Conquistadors in a bloody and appalling travesty of the Christian gospel, but rather the sword of saving truth that leads to the willing embrace of truth, and yet, because others reject the same message, also to division. 'Do not suppose that I have come to bring peace to the earth. I did not come to bring peace, but a sword. For I have come to turn "a man against his father, a daughter against her mother, a daughter-in-law against her mother-in-law – a man's enemies will be the members of his own household"' (Mt 10:34–36).

The gospel of peace is demonstrably divisive because people respond to the message so differently. When Jesus proclaimed peace with God there was always a wide range of reactions: some responded with eagerness and faith; some were attracted but made no settled response; some were indifferent and turned away; some were appalled and schemed how Jesus might die. Every so often I meet Christians who have paid for their conversion with the terrible price of rejection by their families. This is a hard path of peacemaking to walk, for however harsh the rejection, the disciple needs to keep on making the first move, continuing to seek reconciliation. Bill told me that his father had turned him out of the house on the day of his conversion in his early twenties. Every few months he would go back to the house and as he stood by the front door his father would look out from a window and simply shake his head. When he told me the story Bill was nearing sixty, and his father was now in frail health. Bill refused to abandon his quest, but resolutely continued to extend the offer of reconciliation to the stubborn atheist.

All who have discovered and put their trust in the Great Peacemaker are called to the way of peace. Peacemaking is rich with whole-life implications, but there is no disguising the hazardous prospects when we dare to embrace the seventh beatitude. Although Jesus' ministry brought peace to others, it also led inexorably to his rejection and death on the cross. Jesus declared that peacemakers would be called 'sons of God'. This noble and honourable title is high praise indeed, on earth and in heaven. But it is also the description that the centurion used of Jesus, when he saw the manner with which Jesus embraced his crucifixion. No one ever claimed that peacemaking would be a soft option or an easy task. But it is an inescapable dimension of Christ's royal way of love.

Blessed are the persecuted

We have already recognised that Jesus' Beatitudes do not make good sense according to the values that shape today's world. The first seven are remote from the norms of the consumer society that builds itself around the great god of self – 'What's in it for me?' The final beatitude is extreme even by the standards of Jesus' unwavering radicalism. How can anyone possibly be blessed as a direct result of persecution?

Jesus is very specific about the kind of persecution that is blessed. Christians will not secure this blessing through paranoid delusions that everyone is out to persecute them. This is real persecution that Jesus describes. Nor will Christians enjoy this blessing by going out of their way to be so obnoxious that others feel obliged to persecute them. The sole basis for blessed persecution is expressed in two complementary ways: 'because of righteousness' (v.10) and 'because of me' (v.11). This is persecution as a direct result of Christian living and witness, and so Jesus is already beginning to prepare his disciples for the logical consequence of his own death. John records a much more direct explanation towards the end of Jesus' ministry: 'If they persecuted me, they will persecute you also' (Jn 15:20).

Jesus spells out the customary treatment of the prophets, almost suggesting that persecution could be considered a sign of the true prophet. The chances of Jesus' followers escaping persecution begin to look very thin. In the next few generations, such was the extent of the persecution that a Greek word changed its meaning. In the time of Jesus the natural meaning of the word from which we get the word martyr was simply 'witness'. Before long, 'martyr' began to obtain the meaning it continues to have in the English language. When so many were resolute in witness even to the shedding of their blood, to be a 'martyr' began to assume the distinctive connotation of being killed for the faith.

Jesus emphasises the prospect of false accusations, with all kinds of evil likely to be spoken against his followers. In his own trial, the Sanhedrin were desperate to construct a charge sufficient for them to be able to demand capital punishment from Pilate. Several false witnesses failed to agree, and Jesus was accused of wanting to see Herod's temple torn to the ground. Once they had laid the charge of blasphemy against him, they spat in his face and punched him and mocked his refusal to 'prophesy' the names of his torturers. Within a few years, the catalogue of charges against the Christians was quite extraordinary. Tertullian listed the following accusations:

- *Incest* – because Christians called one another 'brother' and 'sister'.
- *Murdering babies and cannibalism* – because Christians

spoke of eating the body and drinking the blood in their worship meetings.

- *Atheism* – because Christians showed neither respect nor fear for the Roman pantheon of gods.
- *Disloyalty to the emperor* – because Christians refused to offer worship to Caesar or make the confession 'Caesar is Lord'.

To this array of charges we can add three more from a list produced by Minucius Felix from his own experience of the courts of the persecutors, for he prosecuted Christians before his own conversion:

- *Irreligion* – because the Christians had neither altars, temples nor priests.
- *Sexual perversions and orgies* – because the Christians met at night.
- *No appreciation of social status* – because the Christians welcomed all as equals. Tatian spelled out the radical equality so despised by the class-conscious snobs of the empire: ' . . . we do not make any distinctions in rank and outward appearance, or wealth and education, or age and sex.'

Unlike the other beatitudes, the eighth has a two-verse clarification attached (Mt 5:11–12). This reinforces the sense of climax and the impression of the inevitability of persecution. The final beatitude identifies the logical consequences of the kingdom of heaven's upside down way of living: not an easy life, let alone endless wealth and success, but rather an almost automatic and universal experience of persecution. The reference to the prophets makes the prospect still more dire, since Jewish tradition suggested that many of the true prophets ended their days murdered by the people who had found their prophecies too demanding.

True to Jesus' words, persecution and martyrdom became

familiar experiences for the early church, often through localised purges of Christians and later through concerted campaigns sanctioned by the more ruthless Caesars. The literature of those early Christian generations lists an horrific array of implements of torture and death. In addition to crucifixion and stoning – the fate of Stephen, the first Christian martyr (Acts 7:54–60) – Nero was said to use Christians as human torches, having them strung up and set on fire to light the imperial gardens of Rome. Other believers suffered in the following ways: burned at the stake; thrown to wild animals; beheaded; tortured with red-hot metal plates; made to sit on an iron chair that had been heated so that they were roasted alive; hung on a post and dangled over wild animals as food; running a gauntlet of whips; rolled over fragments of sea shells that cut the body many times; hung up and flayed, the skin removed with special instruments of torture until the 'anatomy of the body was visible, even to the veins and arteries' (from the Church of Smyrna's letter concerning the persecution and the martyrdom of Polycarp). One man of ninety, Pothinus the overseer of the church at Lugdunun, was dragged before the tribunal and then so brutally kicked and beaten that he collapsed and died two days later.

One of the most renowned of the early martyrs was Polycarp, a revered and elderly church leader from Smyrna. The early stages of interrogation were designed to make the Christian recant. In the case of Polycarp's trial this attempt took the form of demanding that he spoke out in two ways: cursing Christ and 'swearing by the genius of Caesar'. Polycarp was well known, and the crowd denounced him for the impact of his ministry: 'He is the teacher of Asia! The father of the Christians! The destroyer of our gods! He has persuaded many not to sacrifice and not to worship.' Polycarp's response to the threats and entreaties is memorable: 'Eighty-six years have I served him, and he has never done me any harm. How could I blaspheme my King and Saviour?'

They decided to burn Polycarp at the stake. When the mob had brought logs to build the pyre, Polycarp removed his outer clothing and then struggled to take off his shoes. He was old and stiff, and others had taken to removing his shoes for him in his latter years. As was the custom, his executioners wanted to nail him to the stake, but he refused, saying: 'He who gives me strength to endure the fire will also give me the strength to remain at the stake unflinching, without the security of your nails.' The flames failed to take hold of Polycarp's body, and it began to resemble a loaf baking in the oven or a gold bar being refined in a furnace. Eventually the mob could wait no more and demanded that an executioner thrust a dagger into his heart.

Polycarp died in 155, and his church arranged for an eye-witness account of his martyrdom to be written and circulated to other churches for their edification and encouragement. In a remarkable way, persecution and even execution had come to be seen as a privilege, and the deaths of martyrs were related in triumph, not in terror. The promised blessing of Christ had cheated the persecutors even at their moments of ruthless cruelty. The letter from Smyrna summed up the remarkable nobility of the martyrs' deaths:

> Others displayed such heroism that not a cry or a groan escaped from any of them; which seemed a clear proof to us all that in that hour of anguish those martyr heroes of Christ were not present in the body at all – or, better still, that the Lord was standing at their side and holding them in talk. So it was that, with all their thoughts absorbed in the grace of Christ, they made light of the cruelties of this world . . .

Justin Martyr, an early Christian philosopher and evangelist, was martyred in Rome in about 167. He was scourged and beheaded. On trial before the city prefect at the imperial judgement seat, Justin explained why abandoning his faith would be unthinkable, since the future judgement was infinitely more important: 'It is our wish to be martyred for the sake of our Lord Jesus Christ and so be saved. This will be our salvation and our confidence at the much more fearful judgment seat of our Lord and Saviour, who will demand that the whole world comes before his forum.'

The blessed state of martyrdom, promised by Jesus, was plainly experienced by these early Christians, despite the almost unbelievable horror of their deaths and the ease with which they could secure their freedom if they would only denounce Christ and worship Caesar. The first Christians cultivated a quite remarkable buoyancy and resilience. Those in Jerusalem responded to the persecution of the apostles with rejoicing – not with gloom and despondency, nor with urgent prayers that they would never be imprisoned again. Their perspective on the value of life and the privilege of identifying with Jesus is extraordinarily contrary to the self-centred comfort and ease of life that plagues the modern church. Their spiritual worthiness is demonstrated, not by their 'powerful anointing', let alone any aspiration for material prosperity, but rather by their being treated in a similar manner to Jesus at his trial. 'The apostles left the Sanhedrin, rejoicing because they had been counted worthy of suffering disgrace for the Name' (Acts 5:41).

In the West today, persecution has taken on new, more subtle forms. Today's chief weapon against Christians is to patronise or ignore them. It is however still customary to show at least some measure of respect mingled with indifference to every Christian tradition bar one: if someone is known as an 'evangelical' it is fair game to caricature them as a bigoted and brain-dead fundamentalist. Some years ago a new TV channel was about to be launched in Britain and the person in charge of their religious broadcasting came to visit me as a publisher, hoping that I might be able to recommend some contributors. 'We are keen to be fresh, original and creative,' he enthused, rather predictably. 'We want to give opportunities to every religious perspective . . . ' he paused for a moment, then continued, ' . . . except of course to evangelicals like that David Watson. There'll be no place on our channel for that kind of emotional manipulation!' The statement would have been laughable if it had not been so sweepingly dogmatic and completely ignorant. The last thing anyone could possibly have called David Watson was emotionally manipulative. The principle of the eighth beatitude still persists: the way of Jesus is the way of persecution. Misrepresentation is practically certain, and if that is the sum of our persecution, we have got off very lightly indeed.

And so the Beatitudes come to their completion. Anyone who had ascended the hillside to hear about the quiet and happy life must have wondered whether they had already listened for too long. The climax of the Beatitudes provides an astonishing combination of tragedy and triumph, of warning and promise. As Bonhoeffer observed, 'The fellowship of the Beatitudes is the fellowship of the crucified.'

Christian hymns and songs often try to sum up the benefits of Christian living with the superficial hype of a soap powder ad: 'Now I'm happy all the day'; 'I'm H-A-P-P-Y'; 'I'm so happy!' Jesus' great promise in the climax of the Beatitudes is so much more subtle, complex and profound. Those who are prepared to take the risk of living out the Beatitudes will be certain to experience life at its most extreme. They may even experience losing everything, for a life of self-giving love may end in the agony of vicious persecution and martyrdom. And yet they will turn out to have gained everything, receiving in eternity nothing less than the abundant rewards of heaven. Those who are looking for short-term, material and self-centred benefits will find little comfort in Jesus' eight practical steps to a fulfilled and joyous life.

5

Impacting Society –
Living as Salt and Light
Matthew 5:13–16

Living as salt

When Claire and I moved to our present home, we inherited a large garden pond. Neighbourly enquiries revealed that up the road lived the local 'Mr Fish', a man who knew everything that anyone could ever want to know about the care of ponds and their finned occupants. In early spring I went to see him, and to my surprise he immediately offered to sell me a very large bag of salt. I had never seen salt available in such large sacks, and the prospect of adding it to a pond full of freshwater fish seemed quite extraordinary. The only combination of salt and fish with which I was familiar was usually accompanied by batter, vinegar and chips! He patiently explained to me the cleansing properties of salt. After a period of semi-dormancy in winter, fish can be vulnerable to infection in spring because they return to full metabolic activity more slowly than the bacteria and parasites that prey upon them. A dose of salt clears their system and makes them more healthy.

This is just one of the properties of salt with which most of us have become unfamiliar in the modern world. In Ezekiel 16:4 we get a glimpse of ancient midwifery: 'On the day you were born your cord was not cut, nor were you washed with water to make you clean, nor were you rubbed with salt or wrapped in cloths.' The new-born baby was normally rubbed with salt because of its antiseptic qualities, as a form of ancient, preventive medicine. Similarly, those who had suffered injury in the days before antibiotics would have salt rubbed into the wounds, not as a perverse means of provoking extra pain, but because of salt's protective and healing properties.

Salt was also commonly used as a preservative. I was amazed when visiting favelas in Brazil to discover how often those living in shanty towns have made it a priority to own a fridge. Even for the desperately poor, in the modern world the benefit of refrigeration has become one of the bare necessities of life. But in the days before electrical coolants, the only way to enjoy an uninterrupted supply of meat was to have it treated with salt.

The third great virtue of salt is found, of course, in cooking. In health-conscious circles even this use is beginning to be avoided for fear that too much salt in the diet can be harmful, even deadly. Nonetheless, in the hands of a good cook the impact of salt continues to be subtle yet invaluable. Its task is not to trumpet its presence with an astringent blast of saltiness on the palate, but to bring out the flavours of the food. Just as too much salt is overbearing and unpleasant, the complete absence of salt in many dishes is guaranteed to provoke displeasure. For me, most vegetables without salt are bland and almost tasteless. One mouthful is enough to make me add more salt to my own portion without delay.

Salt was therefore a compound of great virtue in the ancient world and considered an absolute necessity in every home. Nothing else combined these three invaluable virtues: to cleanse, to preserve and to savour. Small wonder that tubs of British salt used to declare proudly that Roman soldiers were sometimes even paid in the stuff.

When Jesus compared his disciples with salt, the implications were therefore much richer than the decidedly restricted use of salt in a modern kitchen. Men and women are made in the image of God, and as the salt of the earth the disciples of Jesus are called to bring out that good savour. At the same time, because of human nature's built-in tendency to selfishness, society needs the regular application of moral disinfectant, to purify and preserve.

Once we have begun to understand the life priorities that result from this calling to function as salt, we need to recognise that there are two ways in which we can fail to fulfil our destiny and realise our potential, one implicit and one explicit in the words of Jesus. First, the salt fails to be of benefit if it stays together. In cooking, few things are more unpleasant than a piece of food that has been thoroughly over-salted. The cleansing and curative properties of salt are only available once the salt has been spread out and rubbed in. In Rebecca Manley-Pippert's well-known phrase, the salt must get 'out of the saltshaker'. The purpose of the church is not to withdraw from society into an isolated purity. Of course we need to spend time with our fellow believers – the letter to the Hebrews expressly commands us to make meeting together a continuing priority (Heb 10:25). But the priorities of the New Testament cannot justify our filling every waking hour with church-based activities, seven nights a week. A workaholic treadmill of church activities may help us to be pure, but it will probably make us dull and will certainly make us ineffectual. The only way to fulfil our function as salt is to get spread out and rubbed in. Salt left in the saltshaker is incapable of bringing out the good savour. Nor can it succeed in cleansing and preserving as a moral disinfectant in society.

The second way in which salt can fail is spelled out by Jesus, but is less than obvious in our world. Jesus warns that if salt loses its saltiness, it has become nothing more than useless. In ancient Israel, the standard supply of salt was from the desert region around the Dead Sea, and much of the salt gathered there would have contained impurities. One of the characteristics of salt is that it is extremely soluble: it dissolves in water very quickly. A Jewish family could therefore have a block of Dead Sea salt in the home that would be serving them well, but if it became damp, the pure sodium chloride would quickly disappear, and left behind would be a white compound made up entirely of the impurities. To the eye, it would still look like salt. To the tongue, it would be tasteless and useless. Any Jew who had suffered an invasion of dampness in their home would have known the experience Jesus described. Without warning their salt would have lost its savour.

When Jesus draws a parallel from everyday life, he has a fondness for leaving the implications unexplained. How is it possible for his followers to lose their saltiness? Here the problem is not excessive isolation but its opposite – assimilation into the mainstream of life. Such blending in can be conscious and deliberate or unnoticed and accidental. Either way, the distinctives of discipleship are lost when we settle for the quiet and comfortable life of social conformity. J. B. Phillips' translation of Paul's letter to the Romans captures this habitual tendency and danger for believers in a memorable phrase: 'Don't let the world squeeze you into its mold' (Rom 12:2).

Jesus' consistent call to radical and rigorous discipleship, throughout his teaching and above all in the Sermon on the Mount, is a thoroughgoing repudiation of nominal Christianity. Jesus' concern is not merely that we should attend church on Sunday mornings or give intellectual assent to the words of a creed. He calls us to live as his followers in practice and not just in theory, breaking free from the rigid and constricting conventions of anaemic social conformity.

Although the benefits of salt in the ancient world were

many and obvious, its application was certainly not always pleasant and enjoyable. Some children take pleasure in dipping a wet fingertip into salt and then licking it. With the right quantity of salt, the sharpness on the tongue is almost overpowering and yet pleasurable. In wounds or on the tongue, salt bites. In modern usage, 'rubbing salt into the wound' has negative implications; it suggests putting the boot in, making things worse for someone, taking advantage of their vulnerability. The phrase therefore no longer carries its original meaning, for while the application of salt would be very painful, even agonising, the intention was positive, medicinal and curative.

When Jesus calls us to be salt, the implications are therefore uncomfortable. At times, our lives, values and words will be received by the society in which we live like salt on the tongue or even in a wound. The intention may be positive, but the first impact may be sharp. This is no excuse for abrasiveness or a thundering rant against our opponents, for like Christ himself we must be full of grace as well as truth, demonstrating love's gentleness and mercy even as we express the saltiness of Christian truth. Paul expressed well the integration to which we need to aspire: 'Let your conversation be always full of grace, seasoned with salt' (Col 4:6).

Sadly the church has rarely managed to achieve this attractive but difficult combination. All too often those on the right wing of the church are inclined to go in for mega-decibel denunciations – gunning for all and sundry with words that appear to come from a blunderbuss of super-saturated saltiness. Meanwhile mainline church leaders are faced with a quite different temptation – to sink into a numbing niceness, a saccharine spirituality that is effectively a salt-free zone. Because salt bites, it must be used with care. But if it is never applied, then our supply of salt is of no use at all.

Bearers of light

When we turn to Jesus' second metaphor – light of the world – the properties of light to which Jesus refers are plain. First, *light illumines* and therefore provides safety. In the ancient world a night without a full moon was very dark indeed, unpolluted by the immense amount of light our modern cities continually throw out into the night sky. For Westerners in the electronic age, a dark and unillumined night can seem romantic and exciting. For previous generations, darkness usually spelled danger. People could trip over, lose their way or be subject to attack. One of the medieval churches of the city of York has a curiously broad-set tower, unnecessarily large for church bells and completely open to the elements. In fact this tower was originally the prominent setting for a city beacon so that those journeying across the vale of York could see where the city lay through the gathering gloom of winter fog or the darkness of night.

Light also enlivens. We feel this instinctively in spring, when the first days of brightness and blossom put a new lightness in our step. Today we can understand more clearly this invigorating impact of sunlight, knowing that our skin responds to the sun by producing vitamin D. In northern Russia many people now receive sun lamp treatment in the long, dark months of winter, so that their bodies do not suffer a deficiency of this particular vitamin. In the less severe winters of Britain we can still suffer from a lack of sunlight. Many people find the grey days of February, at the end of our winter, the most difficult part of the year, when emotions dip and depression beckons.

Those who do the cleaning around their home know a further and less welcome aspect of the brighter days of spring: *light exposes*. The sunshine that others may simply enjoy brings to sight every last speck of household dust left unnoticed during winter. That explains the tradition of spring cleaning – the sunlight won't permit any further delay in a thorough dusting and clear out.

Despite the fact that the impact of light is essentially positive, just as salt bites, *light dazzles*. Sometimes when preaching in a large auditorium I have been momentarily blinded by the light, if the stage-lighting is too severe. If someone is kidnapped or taken hostage, they may be blindfolded so that they cannot tell where they have been taken. When the blindfold is finally removed, the sudden glare of sunlight is sure to provoke a rush of pain. Interrogation and torture techniques will sometimes exploit this reaction, often using the harsh glare of a powerful spotlight.

Within the Bible, light is a frequent and highly developed symbol. Light is a prerequisite of life, and God's first action in creation. Light signifies holiness in its unsullied purity. The *shekinah* glory manifests the divine light of God's presence. The promised Messiah will bring light to those who live in darkness. In the New Testament 'light' is one of John's key words: the light of Christ gives life, brings the definitive revelation of God's saving truth, and unmasks the shadow life of human sin and selfishness. The same three strands of meaning are therefore repeated: the light of God is life-giving, truth-revealing and sin-exposing. This light brings both sight and blindness, depending on whether it is met with belief or unbelief. Because it is uncompromisingly pure and exposes all evil, the light of Christ inevitably invites and provokes strong responses, whether joyful acceptance or angry rejection.

Jesus' mini-parable about light is deliberately absurd, as in normal circumstances no one lights a lamp and promptly conceals it. This therefore prompts us to ask why we should be tempted to hide the light. We may hide the light *for fear of persecution*, like Peter during his threefold denial of Christ. We may hide the light *for embarrassment*, not wishing to be associated with others who have behaved foolishly or corruptly while claiming the name of Christ. We may hide the light because *we want to fit in*, whether for the sake of popularity or promotion.

Unfortunately church history reveals that Christians have often been extremely efficient at hiding the light. Kierkegaard once observed that while Jesus turned water into wine, the church has achieved an even greater miracle: turning the wine of Jesus' good news into the water of human religion. We can hide the light within fortified and unwelcoming buildings, or behind impenetrable and archaic religious jargon. We cultivate a nostalgic cultural irrelevance that alienates the great mass of people today. (I have explored these issues at length in my book *21st Century Church*.)

We can certainly hide the light behind trying too hard at evangelism. In that brilliant book we have already mentioned, *Out of the Saltshaker*, Rebecca Manley-Pippert confides that the kind of evangelism practised in some circles is something she wouldn't wish to do to her dog! Some do this through being too pushy and aggressive, others through the cultivation of zealous misery. In a town where I once lived the devoted members of one church were committed to High Street evangelism every Saturday morning. Some cartoon characters walk about with a rain cloud over their heads. If they go indoors the cloud follows and continues to rain upon them. These Christians looked as if they had suffered the same fate. Alarmed passers-by would cross the street rather than risk catching whatever religious misfortune had afflicted these poor, miserable souls.

We can also hide the light by watering down the gospel in order to make it more palatable to our society. Herein lies the consummate failure of twentieth-century liberalism: what they ended up with was a mutation of biblical Christianity, unrecognisable to orthodox believers and unappealing to non-Christians. Even more tragically we hide the light without even realising it, when the compromises and prejudices of our personal lifestyle are more compelling than our words. People cannot hear what we are saying if our lives are shouting a contradictory message.

Jesus' call not to hide the light speaks of lifestyle and words. Our lifestyle needs to demonstrate the light that exposes sin and enlivens with vitality and purity. But our words must explain the meaning of that light, the enlightenment that we have received from the revelation of Christ. Some might object that the witness of their lives is quite sufficient without ever adding words, but this is entirely unrealistic. If Jesus needed to preach and tell parables in order to explain the light of his life, how much more we need to speak out when the witness of our lives is so much more faltering than the blazing purity of the light of the life of Jesus.

In our words we not only explain the gospel and point to Jesus, but we are also called to contend for the truth, guarding the gospel against the false teaching of those who would grievously distort it. We also need to speak out in order to defend or campaign for biblical standards in personal, political and commercial life. The light of the gospel that calls us to personal repentance and living faith also calls us to defend the weak and speak out against society's abandonment of the Ten Commandments.

Downward tendency and serving purpose

Implicit in Jesus' call to be salt and light is a disconcerting, almost bleak, perspective. We are called to be salt and light, not gratuitously – that is, merely on a whim – but because the world desperately needs these qualities. Salt, because the world has a built-in tendency to decay – only with the application of a moral antiseptic can society be cleansed and preserved so that the savour of God's image can be brought out anew. Light, because the world has a built-in tendency to darkness – only as our light shines without apology or compromise can men and women discover the saving source of that light in Jesus Christ.

Whenever a local church degrades into a social club, Christians develop an unambiguous and deeply unattractive attitude: 'What's in it for me?' This terrible question reveals that a disciple has lost their way in unenlightened self-interest. They have become a consumer Christian, evaluating a local church by the same kind of criteria they would apply to a supermarket. Jesus' teaching about salt and light points in the polar opposite direction. He calls his followers to a life centred on others, embracing the reverse of the normal and instinctive human priority which is to look after yourself first.

Our double calling as salt and light sets a clear agenda for the teaching programme of the local church. In order to declare and explain the light, we need a clear grasp of the Bible. A great blight upon the church at the end of the twentieth century is biblical illiteracy. We need to read the Bible not merely to receive a 'verse for the day', but to develop a thoroughgoing Christian mind, richly informed by the truths of Scripture. At the same time, to function properly as salt we need a clear understanding of the issues of the marketplace: the ambitions, priorities and ethical debates of today's world. Local churches need to provide opportunities for Christians to explore issues beyond church, in the world of work (from accounting to the performing arts) and leisure (from sport to shopping), where the vast majority of believers spend most of their time. To function effectively as salt and light we need both to understand our world and to have a clear grasp of the teaching of Scripture. My fear is that many churches are cocooned within an other-worldly pietism, a religious club adrift from and oblivious to the concerns of the surrounding society. Indifference to the world and ignorance of the Bible are a deadly combination. As light we become enfolded in shadows; as salt we become insipid and ineffectual.

From 'I am' to 'you are'

Billy Graham told a story about Mother Teresa shortly after her death. She had been visiting Washington and spoke out clearly at a National Prayer Breakfast about a controversial moral issue. The President of the United States admired her courageous stand and was heard to murmur, 'She's really something! I wish I had a faith like that.' This surely demonstrates the response to our obedience that Jesus foretold. When Christians genuinely and successfully live out their calling as salt and light, even unbelievers will give praise to God for their good works (Mt 5:16).

The most shocking thing about Jesus' teaching on salt and light is the way he transfers something of his own identity to his followers. When Jesus speaks of himself as the light of the world (Jn 8:12), we accept his words unhesitatingly. The Son of God incarnate, with perfect consistency between his teaching and his lifestyle, brings to earth the transcendent light of the Godhead in a way that is revelatory and definitive. There is no one to compare with the Son in his glory – his standing as the light of the world is unique and exclusive.

Perhaps in deference to the uniqueness of Jesus, Christians have tended to misinterpret this section of the Great Sermon. Jesus' two statements have usually been taken as twin imperatives: you must try to be or you need to become salt and light. But Jesus is not merely calling us to make a determined effort. He offers a direct description of our new identity. In the decision to follow Christ, we exercise faith, accepting that he really is the light of life come into the world. As a result of that decision we are implicated in the good news we profess. Our lives and words will influence others either to reject our Master or to join us in following him. More than that, living faith in Christ impacts our inner being. Jesus explains this in terms of the transforming presence of the kingdom of God: as we put our trust in Christ, we submit ourselves to the rule of God and the kingdom arises within us. Paul's complementary explanation is in terms of the Son and the Spirit: through faith in Christ we become a new creation – the old has gone, the new has come – and the Spirit of God indwells us. To have Christ in us, and to be in Christ, mean that his life is dynamically present within us and begins to be seen in our lives and words. By faith in Christ we become, according to Jesus' own teaching, salt as he is salt and light as he is light.

The implication of this remarkable teaching is that discipleship is about more than making a determined and consistent effort to follow Jesus' example. More profoundly we need to discover within ourselves new inward resources in union with Christ. This does nothing to distract from his unique and revelatory status as the Son of God incarnate, but in union with Christ we have a brand new identity. Jesus therefore calls us to an adventure of faith, discovering and seeking to fulfil our astonishing new potential. By choosing to become Jesus' disciples we have actually and already become nothing less than the salt of the earth and the light of the world.

PART TWO

The Way of Perfection
Matthew 5:17–48

6

Jesus' Attitude to the Law
Matthew 5:17–20

In summer 1997 Spring Harvest sent a copy of my book on the Ten Commandments to every MP. Most Christians would unhesitatingly state that the Ten Commandments provide the essential foundation for reversing the moral and spiritual decline of the West. However, when the parliamentary distribution was made public, one correspondent to a denominational newspaper condemned the initiative. Surely, he argued, the Commandments are negative and are therefore completely contradicted by the positive message of Jesus. What's more, since the time of Jesus we have had 2,000 years to evolve morally. The Ten Commandments, he expostulated, were rendered obsolete by the teaching of Jesus and are completely irrelevant to the morally superior men and women of the late twentieth century.

It was difficult to decide which error was more immense: the complete misrepresentation of Jesus' attitude to the Law, or the utterly preposterous assertion that each generation of children is inevitably morally superior to their parents as a direct consequence of the continuing 'moral evolution' of the human race. In technology twentieth-century advances are unprecedented, but there is not the slightest evidence of a parallel and automatic progress towards the ethical high ground.

In the first section of the Great Sermon, which we have entitled 'The way of fulfilment', Jesus gave some remarkably original and radical teaching. This obviously begged a question for his first audience: Did this teaching genuinely flow from the Jewish scriptures, or did it represent an entirely novel religion? As the Christian church became established the question continued to press – Gentile Christians wanted to know how seriously they should take the Old Testament. At the same time, Jewish Christians had to come to terms with the unwelcome reality that most Jews did not join the 'people of the way' and that some of the most vigorous opposition to the proclamation of the young church came from their fellow Jews. Did this rejection demonstrate a fundamental discontinuity between their new-found faith and the ancient religion of their people?

The second section of the Sermon, which we have entitled 'The way of perfection', is enormously important. For Jesus, this is the moment when he reasserts his Jewish credentials and clarifies the relationship between his teaching on the kingdom of heaven and the existing revelation and demands of the Hebrew holy book. For Matthew, whose Jewishness in his concerns and perspective we explored in Chapter 2, this section of Jesus' preaching is vital to establish and demonstrate the right kind of continuity between the old and the new.

Fulfilling the Law and the Prophets (v.17)

An extreme and unacceptable interpretation of Jesus' teaching is expressly contradicted in the first phrase of this new section: 'Do not think that I have come to abolish . . .' (5: 17). The vigour of this repudiation indicates that some Jews were already drawing this conclusion about Jesus' teaching and ministry. At least three possible sources can be identified. First, it could have arisen among Jesus' opponents, who regularly charged him with a casual disregard for the Law and for traditional Jewish interpretations. The Gospels record their strenuous objections to his disciples' consumption of food and his own healing ministry on the sabbath (Mt 12:1–14) and also his relaxed attitude to the traditions of hand-washing and unclean food (Mt 15:20; Mk 7:19). Second, it could have arisen among some of Jesus' disciples, who concluded with misguided zeal that the logical consequence of his radical new approach to holy living was to disregard the Hebrew scriptures completely. Third, this interpretation of Jesus could have arisen among those who grasped the principle of grace, understood that this excluded legalistic attempts to self-righteousness, but then went to the opposite extreme of antinomianism – that is, a complete disregard for any kind of restriction upon personal behaviour (*nomos* = law, so antinomian means anti-law).

Certainly such attitudes did arise in the early church and have continued to plague the church in every generation, for this was the attitude that Bonhoeffer summed up in the phrase 'cheap grace'. Paul's emphatic and persistent rejection of the legalists (usually Judaisers who wanted Gentile Christians to conform in every way to the Old Testament Law) was consistently held in tension with his rejection of the equal and opposite error of lawlessness and a casual disregard for sinful indulgence among the followers of Christ (e.g. Rom 6:1–2; 1 Cor 5).

Whatever the origin of this interpretation of his intentions, Jesus repudiates it entirely. While much of the debate, whether among Jesus' opponents or supporters, would have centred specifically upon the Law, Jesus deliberately uses the wider phrase 'the Law or the Prophets'. In this way, Jesus broadens the debate to insist upon a decisive continuity between his teaching and the whole of the Old Testament.

Throughout this section of teaching, Jesus is weaving his way through a minefield of equal and opposite overstate-ments and misrepresentations with considerable theological sophistication and subtlety. The verb with which Jesus sums up his relationship to the Law is extremely significant – 'I have not come to abolish them but to *fulfil* them' (5:17, my emphasis). The concept of Jesus the fulfiller is very important to Matthew, who uses the verb 'to fulfil' sixteen times, compared with twice by Mark and nine times by Luke. Of these sixteen uses, twelve are connected with ways in which Jesus' life and ministry fulfil specific Old Testament prophecies (1:22; 2:15, 17, 23; 4:14; 8:17; 12:17; 13:35; 21:4; 26:54, 56; 27:9). So if Jesus fulfils the Old Testament in the details of his life, what does it mean more broadly for him to have come to fulfil the Law and the Prophets?

First, Jesus fulfils the Old Testament in his *practical and untarnished obedience*. He enacts the obligations of the Law and Prophets. When the crowds turned against him, they were unable to name a single offence he had committed against the ways of God.

Second, Jesus fulfils the Old Testament by providing the *definitive interpretation of its deepest intentions*. He refutes the superficial piety of the Pharisees, with their legalistic obsession with outward conformity, through his distinctive emphasis on purity of heart and self-giving love.

Third, Jesus fulfils the Old Testament by *completing the revelation* thus far provided. He goes beyond the teaching of previous generations and gives final, definitive form to God's intentions for the human race.

Fourth, and above all, Jesus fulfils the Old Testament because *in his person he represents the promises fulfilled*. All the purposes, longings and aspirations of the Hebrew scriptures come to focus in his life and ministry.

This fourth level of meaning in the verb 'to fulfil' is unmistakably apparent in Matthew's regular use of the verb and it had profound, indeed revolutionary, consequences for the disciples of Jesus. At first Jesus' Jewish audience naturally and properly wanted to interpret and evaluate his life and teaching in the light of the scriptures, which were the given and objective yardstick by which to assess the man and his teaching. Once Jesus was recognised as the great and promised one who fulfilled the scriptures, the order of priority was reversed, for a new centre of gravity had been found. It was no longer Jesus who must be interpreted in the light of the Law and the Prophets, but rather the Hebrew scriptures must now be interpreted in the light of Jesus.

To fulfil the Law and the Prophets is therefore to affirm their importance and validity. They must not be despised or discarded lightly. And yet at the same time, this fulfilment relativises their authority. In an unprecedented way the sacred writings must yield centre stage to the one whose coming they have anticipated. In his person and teaching, Jesus claims to provide nothing less than the definitive revelation of God, the complete embodiment of the requirements and aspirations of the Law and the Prophets.

Beyond the Gospels, the New Testament contains a great deal of further exploration of ways in which Jesus' life and death fulfilled the Old Testament. Matthew includes a saying of Jesus that was designed to provoke such reflection: 'The Son of Man did not come to be served, but to serve, and to give his life as a ransom for many' (Mt 20:28). Peter came to recognise that Jesus' reaction to imminent death fulfilled the promise of the suffering servant in Isaiah 53. Peter quotes Isaiah both directly and indirectly as he goes on to affirm the redemptive power of Jesus' death (1 Pet 2:21–25). The letter to the Hebrews explores at length the ways in which Jesus' death fulfils the ultimate intentions of the ritual and sacrificial laws of the Old Testament. There is continuity – a priest and a sacrifice – but also radical discontinuity – the death of Christ is once for all, an atoning sacrifice so complete that all other sacrifices are superfluous, with the result that the entire Jewish sacrificial system has been rendered obsolete (e.g. Heb 9:11–15).

Above all, Paul is the great New Testament theologian of the cross, which he made absolutely central to his preaching (1 Cor 2:2). Although in his life Jesus uniquely fulfilled the Law in perfect obedience, in his death on a tree he came under the Law's curse (Gal 3:13). This was no accident, but fulfilled the double purpose of God, who needed to fulfil his own righteousness, having delayed a full response in righteous judgement to human sin, and who simultaneously needed to take effective action to rescue the human race from the necessary and inevitable consequences of our offences against his law (Rom 3:25–26). Jesus therefore fulfils the Law both in his life and in his death, where he becomes for us the atoning sacrifice. What's more, this transaction of grace does more than provide forgiveness, for we can freely receive 'the righteousness that comes from God and is by faith' (Phil 3:9). Nothing less than Jesus Christ's own perfect and right standing before the Father is granted to us, not by law but by grace. The ultimate fulfilment of the Old Testament is found therefore in the righteousness of Christ that is imputed to believers who are incapable of attaining such a standing before God by means of our own faltering and flawed obedience. What was impossible by human effort is fully accomplished by divine grace. The Old Covenant is not casually disregarded, but rather completed and transcended in the death and resurrection of Christ: 'For it is by grace you have been saved, through faith – and this not from yourselves, it is the gift of God – not by works, so that no-one can boast' (Eph 2:8–9).

The Law's abiding importance (v.18)

Having denied the charge that he planned to abolish the Hebrew scriptures, Jesus underlines his commitment to the

Law. First he affirms its endurance – it will continue as the authoritative revelation of God's requirements until the end of the age. Then he goes further, affirming every last detail down to the iota (the smallest letter in Hebrew) and the hook (the ornamental touch added to some Hebrew consonants). In modern typefaces, serif fonts are those with decorative touches, whereas the sanserif (like this) are the simpler styles. A modern serif is today's closest equivalent to a Hebrew hook. Jesus' claim is deliberately emphatic. He combines two synonymous rabbinic phrases – one referring to a hook, the other to an iota. Matthew strengthens this emphasis in Greek by repeating the numeral – not *one* iota, not *one* hook. Jesus is therefore not only asserting the indestructibility of the Law, agreeing with the rabbinic tradition, but he is also affirming its continued validity and even its verbal inspiration. The Law is inviolate, and cannot be sweepingly disregarded by the followers of Jesus, not merely in its general intent but even in its tiny details.

Nonetheless, even as Jesus affirms the continued authority of the Law, there is a calculated ambiguity in his words. At first Jesus declares that the Law in every last detail will abide until heaven and earth disappear. In general Jewish usage, this phrase simply meant the Law would abide for ever. In the New Testament, this phrase about heaven and earth was understood in a more apocalyptic sense and was connected with the return of Christ: 'Heaven and earth will pass away, but my words will never pass away' (Mt 24:35). Jesus therefore resoundingly affirmed the endurance of the Law, and yet set a time limit upon its authority, in contrast with his own teaching.

At the end of this subtle and extremely telling sentence, Jesus uses a phrase that at first sight seems superfluous: 'until everything is accomplished' (Mt 5:18). Is this tautological, merely another way of reaffirming the enduring status of the

Law, meaning nothing different from the initial phrase about heaven and earth? It could be. And yet Jesus never used words carelessly, any more than Matthew is casual or repetitious in his compilation of Jesus' teaching. The phrase begs a question: When will everything be accomplished, and could the moment of accomplishment be said to occur before the end of the age? If the phrase indicates the ultimate completion of human history, then it cannot signify anything other than the end of the age. But Jesus has already made a remarkable claim for his own significance by saying that he does not merely obey the Law as a faithful Jew, but rather he fulfils it. In his life, therefore, the new age of the kingdom of heaven is dawning: *his perfect obedience* consummates the age of the Law; *his unique standing* as the one who fulfils the Law gives a new and authoritative framework of interpretation to the existing revelation; *his redemptive sacrifice* satisfies the demands of the Law.

Jesus' phrase about everything being accomplished therefore shifts his emphasis in a remarkable way, with implications that could not have been fully understood by his original audience. On the one hand, the Law is the definitive verbal revelation of God's holy purposes for the human race, and these demands will remain undiminished for ever. Simultaneously, inasmuch as the ultimate intentions of the Law have been accomplished in Jesus' life and death, the Law's meaning has become subject to Jesus' definitive interpretation, and its demands are subordinated to Jesus' call to discipleship. The Law's function is therefore abiding and yet preparatory: it is Jesus who has the last word, providing not only the ultimate call to righteousness but also, through his atoning death, the means of becoming right with God. Jesus therefore establishes a profound continuity and an equally profound discontinuity with the age of the Law.

Beyond the Law (vv.19–20)

In this carefully balanced and nuanced defence of both the continuing authority of the Law and yet his own transcendence of it, Jesus again repudiates any antinomian tendencies among his followers. Any excesses of lawlessness or even casual attitudes towards unholy living are without excuse. The warning is twofold, addressing not only our personal behaviour, but also how we teach others. Jesus' concern about teaching should be understood in its broadest sense. If local church ministers and denominational leaders condone law-breaking, they are culpable for the sins of others. At the same time, the attitudes or behaviour of mature disciples may set a bad example or give implicit permission to younger believers to indulge the sinful nature.

Then comes the crunch. Some complained, and others may even have hoped, that Jesus was abolishing the demands of the Law. Certainly the Pharisees considered Jesus and his disciples to be slipshod in their pursuit of holiness: healing on the sabbath and claiming the freedom to eat without ritual hand-washing. But now Jesus makes two outrageous claims. First, far from settling for an easy life in contrast with the misplaced zealous legalism of the Pharisees, Jesus insists that our righteousness must exceed that of the Pharisees. Second, such righteousness is the necessary pre-condition of entry to the kingdom of heaven.

Turning first to the means of entry to the kingdom of heaven, Jesus' astonishing and extreme pre-condition is a counsel of perfection and therefore of despair. So far as the Pharisees were concerned, they were the most religious, the most morally scrupulous, of all Jews. They would not even mix with the ordinary people for fear of moral and spiritual contamination – such people were beyond the pale, without hope of ever attaining righteousness. In the crowd that is now listening to his preaching, Jesus addresses these ordinary people, many of whom would have needed no persuading of their own moral deficiencies and spiritual limitations. Without compromise, Jesus demands that they attain the moral high ground, not as a long-term aspiration, the ultimate goal in a life of discipleship, but as the pre-condition for entry to the kingdom.

Where can such absolute righteousness possibly be found? There is surely only one plausible means of satisfying these high demands of access to the kingdom, and it is summed up so clearly and succinctly in Paul's letter to the Philippians: '. . . not having a righteousness of my own that comes from the law, but that which is through faith in Christ – the righteousness that comes from God and is by faith' (Phil 3:9).

What is obtained by faith must then be expressed in the lifestyle of discipleship. So what does it mean to exceed the righteousness of the Pharisees? Once again Jesus rules out the twin extremes that have so often beset the church: the moral carelessness of antinomianism and the legalistic negativity of Pharisaism. The compliment to his adversaries is a backhander, for while Jesus calls his disciples to emulate the zeal and determination of the Pharisees, their concept of righteousness is entirely repudiated. Two kinds of Christian have completely missed Jesus' point: those whose lack of moral resolve has made them indistinguishable from the world, and those whose zeal has been misdirected, causing them to become indistinguishable from the Pharisees in their legalistic negativity.

What follows in the rest of the second section of the Great Sermon (Mt 5:21–48) is Jesus' exploration of what this higher righteousness actually looks like in practice. The righteousness that Jesus champions and exemplifies goes way beyond the merely outward strictures of the legalists. Far from playing down the demands of righteousness or conforming to the customary approach of the Pharisees,

Jesus spells out the extraordinary implications of his messianic intensification of the Law. The alternative lifestyle of the kingdom of heaven depends upon Jesus' thoroughgoing rejection of the rabbinical traditions and his reinterpretation of the ultimate intentions of the Law. The whole-life discipleship which Jesus requires has completely redefined righteousness in terms of his new, messianic priorities of purity of heart and self-giving love.

7

Messianic Intensifications
(a) Anger, Adultery and Divorce
Matthew 5:21–32

The Ten Commandments are the pinnacle of Old Testament ethics, the most succinct and complete moral code ever composed in any society or religion. Anyone who looks at them objectively, Jew or Gentile, believer or unbeliever, is likely to draw the same conclusion. They accurately reflect the moral framework that has been built into the human condition, and it therefore makes good sense to treat them as a universal foundation for any civilised society. The new righteousness of the Sermon on the Mount could not be more different. Jesus' messianic intensifications are extreme and absolutist. In a world that often proves selfish, even ruthless, Jesus' commendation of kingdom living is an affront to the common-sense priorities of self-reliance and self-preservation that normally govern human existence. Without a faith response to the Teacher, the lifestyle of discipleship that Jesus commends seems so extreme as to be absurd.

Once Jesus has made the remarkable claim that his followers' righteousness must exceed that of the Pharisees, he accepts the obligation to explore what such righteousness looks like in practice. In the rest of Matthew 5 Jesus explores six key aspects of this alternative way of living, not to provide an exhaustive account of the new righteousness, but rather to demonstrate the kind of priorities he wants his disciples to pursue.

In each of these six examples Jesus adheres to the same basic structure. First, he quotes an existing moral precept introduced by one of two phrases, either 'You have heard that it was said' or 'It has been said' (5:21, 27, 31, 33, 38, 43). The fullest form of this phrase is used to introduce the first and fourth of the antitheses – 'You have heard that it was said to the people long ago' – which conveniently sub-divides the six into two groups of three, an arrangement we will follow in this and the next chapter. Second, on each occasion Jesus then presents his new righteousness, always beginning with the same phrase: 'But I tell you' (5:22, 28, 32, 34, 39, 44). This represents an extraordinary claim to authority. Rabbis were entitled to express their own opinion, or quote from the scriptures or the rabbinical tradition. Old Testament prophets claimed to report a direct revelation from God – 'Thus says the Lord . . .' But Jesus speaks directly in the first person, claiming to speak with an unassailable authority – the first person of the supreme and unique representative of God on earth.

The stylistic structure of these stark contrasts – 'You have heard . . . But I say' – makes an implicit claim for the person of Jesus. He is someone greater than either Moses or the prophets, let alone the most revered of men in the rabbinical tradition. At the same time, this structure makes an extraordinary claim for the ethical statements that Jesus makes. Here is no judicious and constructive contribution to a continuing ethical debate. Rather, Jesus presents his own perspective as the permanent and definitive, non-negotiable and ultimate moral teaching.

The third distinctive quality found in the sixfold repetition of this structural device is the way in which Jesus consistently implicates his hearers: 'But I tell *you*.' To be sure this provokes questions about Jesus' identity in the manner of so much of his teaching – 'But what about you? Who do *you* say I am?' (Mt 16:15, my emphasis). Beyond our initial appraisal and subsequent faith response to Jesus, the uncompromising authority of these six sets of moral imperatives demands a single-minded and dedicated life of discipleship. The new righteousness calls us to a continuing response of faith to Jesus and obedience to his teaching.

As to the relationship between the original quotations and Jesus' new perspective, there is considerable variation in his approach. Of the six initial quotations, three are taken directly from the Old Testament, two are fair summaries or clarifications of Old Testament teaching, and one gravely distorts the Old Testament. Of Jesus' reinterpretations, three intensify the existing Law without denying its more immediately obvious meaning (murder, adultery and oaths), while three overthrow the natural force of the legislation or tradition that Jesus is quoting (divorce, retaliation and attitudes to enemies).

Although these six examples have been termed 'the messianic antitheses', this diversity in Jesus' handling of the earlier teaching means that they are more accurately described as 'messianic intensifications'. As soon as we look beyond the formulaic simplicity of the repetitive structure, Jesus' intentions are seen to be multiple and complex: he dispenses outright with the authority of the rabbinical tradition; he excludes the methodology of legalism; and he transcends the literal demands of the Old Testament Law, calling people to a religion of the heart and to an accountability to God in the inner hiddenness of life in ways that are entirely beyond external legislation or enforcement.

These six intensifications can be seen as Jesus' practical exposition of the Old Testament love commands. When tested by an expert in the Law, Jesus confidently claimed

that all the Law and the Prophets hung on two commandments, which he quoted from Deuteronomy 6:5 and Leviticus 19:18: '"Love the Lord your God with all your heart
and with all your soul and with all your mind." This is the
first and greatest commandment. And the second is like it:
"Love your neighbour as yourself"' (Mt 22:37–38).

There is however a characteristic extremism to Jesus'
exposition. The mini-parables of this section of the Great
Sermon use the typically extravagant language of Jesus' parables, which leads to problems of interpretation and application – what does Jesus really ask of his followers in practice?
On the one hand, those who attempt a literal and naive
obedience can quickly slip into bizarre behaviour – a red-
blooded fanaticism which is unyieldingly harsh and unpar-
alleled in Jesus' own life. On the other hand, and this is
certainly the more frequent tendency in Western Christianity, those whose interpretation is more sophisticated, who
recognise the hyperbolic intent and impact of Jesus' language, make measured adjustments in terms of what Jesus'
radicalism might mean in the real world. The end result, all
too often, is a learned endorsement of bourgeois respectability, kind and compassionate to be sure, but safe, sterile and
bloodless. Perhaps more than anywhere else in the New
Testament, Jesus' messianic intensifications of the Law
make profound and complex demands upon his interpreters.
We need strenuously to avoid two equal and opposite errors
– naive enthusiasm and sophisticated detachment – for they
both so easily produce a parody, a mutation or a dilution of
the new righteousness which Jesus so vigorously commends.

Beyond murder and anger

Jesus begins his exploration of the new, higher righteousness
by quoting the sixth of the Ten Commandments, against
murder. This is followed by a summary of the consequences

within Judaism, namely legal proceedings before a court. Jesus has no argument with such a response, but his concern is to raise the stakes concerning two ways in which relationships can break down that were too minor for such prosecutions; that is, anger and name calling.

Anger takes different forms according to our personality type. There are the brooders, who may simmer for years with a secret store of bile. There are the exploders, who are spontaneously combustible at regular intervals, perhaps to the accompaniment of crashing crockery. There are the safety-valve eruptors, who let off steam when they experience an overload of stress, not necessarily in the direction of the original stressor. And there are the sergeant majors, who use anger in a calculated way to dominate and manipulate others through a climate of fear.

Although Jesus uses the same phrase for the consequences of anger as was traditionally used for the consequences of murder – 'subject to judgment' – the natural implication is that he is not attempting to propose a new law for the statute book, nor set up a new court of human law, but is rather warning that, whether our anger has been frequently displayed or successfully concealed, in God's final judgement we will have to face the dread consequences. Anger and verbal abuse are usually accepted as inevitable aspects of life. The best thing to do is to cultivate a thick skin to avoid getting hurt. They are minor irritations that should not be taken too seriously. Jesus therefore vigorously repudiates the way in which his fellow Jews had trivialised such offences. For him, they are nothing less than a fundamental breach of the love command. This doesn't mean that Jesus flattens out morality, as if to suggest that a moment of anger deserves exactly the same punishment as murder, but he extends the demands of his higher righteousness to exclude socially acceptable and everyday expressions of hot temper or bile.

Clearly some early copyists found Jesus' absolute exclusion of anger too extreme and unrealistic, so they inserted a qualifying phrase – 'angry *without cause*'. This let-out clause is clearly later and has no basis in the teaching of Jesus. But what about Jesus' expulsion of the traders from the Temple precincts (Mt 21:12)? This has often been described as 'righteous anger'. To be sure, when Jesus brandished a whip, overturned the money-changers' tables and drove them out, he was hardly behaving with the cool and prim politeness of an English functionary: 'I am most terribly sorry, but I'm afraid I must ask you if you would be so kind as to vacate this area as soon as possible. Thank you so much.' There is, however, no cruelty, no loss of control evident in Jesus; no actions or words that he would later regret. He purges the parasites with the efficiency of a vet eradicating fleas from a dog. He does what righteousness demands must be done – a prophetic act of exclusion from the Temple, reasserting its role as a house of prayer – but there is no incandescent rage, no hot-headedness in the behaviour of Jesus. Those who claim the precedent of 'righteous anger' for their own attitudes run a very grave risk of being altogether less controlled and pure in their motivation, words and actions. The example of Jesus gives not the slightest legitimacy to venomous misrepresentation of others or to any indulgence of vindictiveness or fury.

Jesus specifically refers to someone's anger 'with his brother'. In fact there are four references to 'brothers' in three verses (5:22 – twice, 23, 24). Most murders do occur within the family, so Jesus may be using the word in its general meaning, whether indicating a close relative or referring more broadly to any fellow human being. However, given the early Christian fondness for describing one another as 'brother and sister', the natural, primary meaning of 'angry with his brother' among the churches for whom Matthew was writing would have been 'angry with a fellow disciple'. This emphasis underlines Jesus' conviction that discipleship finds its full expression within a community of believers and clearly condemns sectarian hostility towards non-believers. There is a similar emphasis in Jesus' new love command. The Old Testament provides the universal and inclusive instruction to love our neighbours as ourselves, but Jesus gives his disciples a new measure for their mutual love: 'As I have loved you, so you must love one another' (Jn 13:34). John develops this same theme in his first letter, with the warning that we truly love God with the measure of love that we have for the 'brother' (here unambiguously a fellow Christian) whom we love the least: 'If anyone says, "I love God," yet hates his brother, he is a liar. For anyone who does not love his brother, whom he has seen, cannot love God, whom he has not seen' (1 Jn 4:20).

The quest for a righteousness that exceeds that of the Pharisees makes constant demands upon our relationships. It is not enough to avoid committing murder. Jesus calls us to the higher path of learning to evict anger and hatred from our innermost being, both in our general dealings with others and in particular in our relationships with fellow believers.

Once Jesus has established this general principle of profound intolerance to anger, leaving us no excuse for natural, instinctive, normal human responses, he emphasises the rigour of his new righteousness with reference to name calling and then uses two examples to illustrate the priority of the new righteousness: not merely avoiding negative emotion, but actively pursuing reconciliation. Turning to name calling, Matthew uses two words, one Aramaic and one Greek. *Raca* means imbecile, and was considered greatly offensive among the Jews. Although it could be used in the context of excommunication when one rabbi denounced another, in other circumstances anyone who used it was, as Jesus indicates, subject to a disciplinary court.

The Greek word *moros* literally meant the same as *raca*, as reflected in the modern English use of 'moron' as a similar term of abuse. To Jewish ears it probably had the additional implication of being a spiritual outcast – not merely mentally defective.

Jesus is forbidding all kinds of insult, whether casual or inflamed with anger, that treat an opponent as less than fully human, whether that involves impugning their intellectual capabilities or their spiritual state. When Jesus' approach is so rigorous concerning abuse that refers to intellectual capacity and spiritual status, we should logically apply the same standards to other categories of name calling: people are demeaned by derogatory language that is contemptuous of their gender, the colour of their skin, their social class or their physical disability. Every expression of contempt that treats its victims with less than human dignity is without excuse for the disciples of higher righteousness.

The implications of Jesus' teaching can be pressed still further, because in the Greek catalogue of abusive vocabulary, *moros* was by no means the most offensive or graphic of insults. Like the use of 'fool' in modern English – 'Don't be such a fool!'; 'You are a fool!' – *moros* was a moderate and fairly socially acceptable form of abuse. Jesus may therefore be condemning the very act of using any kind of abusive language, however mild or casual, humorous or intentionally inoffensive. All verbal abuse, whether devastating or trivial, needs to be seen as a breach of the second great love command and entirely intolerable among those who aspire to the higher righteousness of the Sermon on the Mount.

Jesus completes his intensification of the command against murder by moving from strictures against anger and verbal abuse to a commendation through two mini-parables of the virtue of reconciliation. Jesus expects his followers not merely to avoid committing murder as the ultimate breakdown of human relations, nor even simply to eschew anger and name calling, but to be actively committed to reconciliation. If the cultivation of anger may ultimately lead to murder, its repudiation should make Jesus' disciples into relationship-menders.

In the first mini-parable, Jesus emphasises the active pursuit of reconciliation. It portrays someone who is in the very act of presenting their gift at the altar when they suddenly abandon their offering in order first to secure reconciliation. The illustration is extreme: modern equivalents might be leaving your baby in the hands of a minister at a dedication or baptism, or even interrupting your wedding service in order first to patch up an argument with a brother or sister. Jesus' illustration is calculated in its extremism. Common sense might suggest that if reconciliation is so important it should become our first priority once the presentation of the offering has been completed. But Jesus is arguing that no acts of religious piety are more important than reconciliation, and even, implicitly, that God is more concerned about our relationships than our offerings; lavish financial donations cannot conceal or compensate for the relationships that we choose to break. Jesus also emphasises the need to make the first move: whoever has caused the breach, every disciple is commanded to be a mender of relationships.

Turning to the second mini-parable, the previous difficult relationship was with a 'brother', but this time it is with an 'adversary'. By implication, the believer is now in a legal conflict with an unbeliever who has no hesitation in securing full recompense for every wrong, including imprisonment and punitive financial compensation. The emphasis is not upon a full restoration of a positive relationship, but Jesus nonetheless urges us to take the initiative in damage limitation, resolving the dispute as best we can. At first sight, the

second mini-parable is therefore a straightforward commendation of prudent behaviour: settle legal disputes quickly
because delay is always likely to make things worse.

The theme of urgency establishes a connection between
the two mini-parables: the person with the offering must
leave it behind without completing the presentation; the
person with an adversary must settle the matter with equal
haste. This characteristic emphasis underlines the pressing
priority of reconciliation – this is not an initiative that we can
keep delaying. It also reflects the general sense of imminence
in Jesus' teaching on the kingdom of heaven. Now is the
time when God's kingdom is at hand. Now is the time to
repent and believe. Now is also the acceptable hour for the
active pursuit of reconciliation. The inbreaking of the kingdom of heaven requires us never to leave till tomorrow the
reconciliation we could pursue today.

Beyond adultery and lust

The second intensification is the least complex. Jesus begins
by quoting the seventh of the Ten Commandments, against
adultery, and to this he adds a new offence: committing
adultery in the heart. In these first two intensifications Jesus
has addressed the two major arenas of broken relationships:
murder and adultery. Today's headlines confirm the abiding
power and destructiveness of these twin excesses. But Jesus
relentlessly pursues the motivation behind these outward
sins into the hidden attitudes of anger and lust.

Some early Christian writers assumed that sexuality was
intrinsically sinful. This led to the medieval assumption that
those who were married and sexually active were by definition spiritually compromised. Therefore, they argued, only
those who were celibate and single could become priests,
monks or nuns. Such a line of argument simply cannot be
found in the New Testament. These Christian thinkers were

influenced less by the Bible than by the high culture of the Graeco-Roman world. In particular, they accepted the dualistic anthropology of Platonism, which elevated mind, reason and spirit, but reduced our bodies, mortality and sexuality to the lower plane of human existence. Within the Old Testament, sexuality and love-making are presented in Genesis 1 and 2 as wholesome, positive gifts of God in creation. The Song of Songs celebrates the gift of sexual love. There is nothing in the Old Testament or the New to suggest that Jesus was roundly condemning as sinful any and every experience of sexual attraction.

The Greek word for 'woman' in verse 28 is almost always used of married women. We could therefore translate the verse as condemning anyone who looks lustfully at another man's wife. But this is to narrow the implications of Jesus' teaching too far. The key word is 'lustfully', which literally means 'in order to desire her in a forbidden way'. In its broadest sense this verse therefore condemns not only all acts of adulterous sex and sex outside marriage, but also any tendency to allow the imagination to dwell on such prospects.

Such attitudes are positively encouraged in many settings. My first Saturday job as a teenager not only provided me with a huge number of dirty jokes, but every woman who passed the shop window was professionally evaluated by the senior male staff, giving her a mark out of ten as a sex object. Such attitudes are summed up in the expression 'undressing her with his eyes'. It is also perfectly possible to look at someone lustfully without depersonalising them, for the feelings of sexual attraction may be reciprocated and encouraged. On more than one occasion I have had to deal pastorally with an adulterous relationship that has begun when a couple started confiding in one another to a greater degree than with their marriage partners. This easily spills over into criticising the spouse – 'I'm just not understood or appreciated at home.' Before they know it, the couple have set their relationship on a slippery slope that leads towards full-blown adultery.

So is it possible to experience sexual attraction without lust? Yes, of course, for sexual attraction is a wholesome prelude to marriage. Sexuality in itself is not an expression of our sinfulness but of our humanity. To appreciate someone's personality, to enjoy their company, to admire their good looks, these are all intrinsic parts of positive human relationships. A look becomes lustful when it moves from appreciation to a desire for sexual possession, and that is what Jesus condemns.

Jesus' intensification of the Law on adultery is much stricter than our society can bear, but not as narrow as those Christians who propose that our sexuality is intrinsically sinful or dirty. The great art galleries of the Vatican contain many nude statues to which fig leaves were later added by official Catholic decree. While some modern representations of the nude are avowedly pornographic, with the express intention of provoking lustfulness, fig leaves are not a necessary consequence of Jesus' teaching. If an individual is unable to look at any representation of the human nude without being overwhelmed with lust, they should avoid visiting art galleries, but those who can appreciate the beauty of the human form without such trauma are entirely free to do so.

Jesus' teaching inevitably raises the question of whether women are ever responsible for stirring lustful thoughts. It remains one of the standard defences in rape cases that the victim provoked the attack by her clothes and manner. In all but the most extreme circumstances, such a line of defence is contemptible, for clothing and conversation are no justification for sexual violation. The fundamentalist Muslim solution to the problem of male lust is to enforce total covering upon their women, whose eyes and hands alone can be seen by other men. When men are free to wear what they want, this is an appalling infringement of human rights, a tyranny by gender against which Christians should strenuously object. In southern Europe, women tourists are not allowed to enter a Roman Catholic church unless their knees and shoulders are covered, which has always seemed to me a rather arbitrary way of excluding 'immodest dress'. Nonetheless, while such sanctions are oppressive, arbitrary and extreme, since Jesus' second intensification is particularly directed to men, there must be some measure of responsibility upon women not to be needlessly provocative. Some extremes of fashionable clothing are so revealing, so sexually provocative, that it is quite difficult for a man to know where to turn his gaze.

From this general principle of rejecting lustful thoughts as well as the act of adultery, Jesus turns to two parallel applications. These take the form of an almost identical pair of mini-parables. The offending eye should be gouged out and discarded and the offending hand should be cut off and discarded, for in both cases self-amputation is better than the whole body being thrown into hell. Jesus probably refers to the right eye and the right hand for the simple reason that, by cultural tradition and because most people are right-handed, the right side is seen to be stronger, more useful. This is the eye or hand that we would normally be most concerned to protect and preserve. It seems almost inconceivable today, but Origen, a great early church theologian, was said to have castrated himself in response to Jesus' teaching. The fact that he was not alone in considering such a course of action is demonstrated by the Council of Nicea in 325, which expressly prohibited such behaviour among over-zealous believers.

Self-mutilation is arrant folly, with no justification in Jesus' teaching. His words are plainly metaphorical and deliberately, even extravagantly, overstate the necessary corrective action in order to emphasise the seriousness of sexual sin. His intention is not to produce a generation of self-disabled disciples, but rather to shock his hearers out of their complacent toleration of lustful fantasies. Jesus' original target was not those influenced by Platonism, who thought that all sexuality was automatically dirty and sinful, but rather those who could see no harm in letting their imagination run riot in sexual fantasies so long as they avoided actual adultery. A woman I know was working in the Middle East and she told me of the contemptuous and animalistic stares with which men casually assaulted her in everyday life. Jesus allows no tolerance or excuse for such behaviour.

In a sex-saturated society, images of sexual invitation and incitement to lust are found on many street corners, in many newspapers and magazines, and even in the telephone kiosks of major cities, where prostitutes unashamedly tout their wares. Our culture is not geared up to the appreciation of beauty, but to the availability of casual sex. The world in which we live is at least as inclined to promote lustful thoughts as the Roman Empire of the time of Jesus; his unequivocal exclusion of lust is as shocking to our society as it was to first-century Galilee. The believer who takes Jesus' words seriously will know what it is to walk the knife edge between the positive affirmation of human sexuality and the destructive consequences of giving house room to lustful thoughts. What we need to retain is Jesus' concern with the priority of purity, destroying or fleeing from all incitements and cutting off all opportunities that will drag us down into lustful self-indulgence.

Beyond casual divorce

The third messianic intensification is very different from the first two. Jesus' exclusion of anger and lustful thoughts prompts his disciples to self-examination, recognising that no one else but God can know the secrets of our inner life. However, Jesus' teaching on marriage is unavoidably in the public arena, affecting the covenant relationship of every married person who wants to respond to his call to a higher righteousness.

Jesus' opening quotation is from the Mosaic Law (Deut 24:1), which gave practical instructions about what to do following a divorce. The breakdown of marriage is certainly not encouraged or treated lightly in the Old Testament, but is rather recognised as an unfortunate fact, a living reality in response to which appropriate legislation needs to be formulated. Strictly speaking, what Moses commands is not divorce as such, but two consequences of marital breakdown: first that a man must issue his wife with a certificate of divorce, thus formally cancelling the marriage bond once it has been broken (Deut 24:1); and second, that if a woman remarries and her second husband subsequently dies or also divorces her, then she and her first husband are not allowed to remarry (Deut 24:4).

By the time of Jesus, the emphasis of Deuteronomy had been significantly distorted, so that Moses was understood to have 'commanded' divorce itself, not merely the provision of a formal certificate in the event of divorce. This was the interpretation offered by the Pharisees in their dispute with Jesus, which Matthew records in a later and more developed account of Jesus' teaching on marriage (Mt 19:1–9). Jesus corrects the current interpretation, explaining that Moses 'permitted' divorce. He therefore treats the divorce clauses in the Law as a reluctant concession by Moses, 'because your hearts were hard'. In defining the essential nature and purpose of marriage, Jesus looks behind the Law, choosing to begin not with Moses' permission but with the divine ideal expressed in Genesis 2:24. In reasserting this ideal, Jesus defends the sanctity of marriage as a lifelong, exclusive covenant relationship: 'Therefore what God has joined together, let man not separate' (Mt 19:6).

Since the Mosaic Law had already accepted the reality of marital breakdown, the rabbinical tradition had debated the legitimate grounds for divorce, proposing radically different interpretations of the key word 'indecency' in Deuteronomy 24:1. While the school of Shammai only allowed divorce on grounds of proven adultery, the school of Hillel gave men almost entirely unrestricted access to divorce, so that they could divorce their wife for an offence as small as talking to another man or burning a meal. There was no court involved – a man could simply announce his divorce, hand over the certificate required by Moses and the marriage was at an end. In Jesus' time, Hillel's interpretation held sway, so divorce was easy and casual. Roman rule only intervened in cases of premarital sex and adultery, where Jewish Law imposed a sentence of death, and the Empire did not permit this capital punishment to be enacted.

In this climate of casual divorce, Jesus explains the logical consequences. If a Jewish woman is divorced, her remarriage is a practical inevitability, so Jesus warns that a man who casually divorces his wife imposes upon her the automatic status of an adulterer (Mt 5:32). She is not the only one to come under judgement: the man who marries her will also become an adulterer (Mt 5:32), as will her former husband if he then chooses to remarry (Mt 19:9). The logic is plain, even though the demands are harsh: when marriage is intended to be for life, any subsequent sexual union that cuts across that marriage covenant is by definition adulterous.

Only two exceptions to this rigorous approach are permitted. First, the Jews accepted that since marriage is intended to be for life, the death of a spouse concludes the marriage bond and the surviving partner is entirely free to marry again. Second, these strict prohibitions of divorce do not apply if circumstances can be identified in which the divorce can be sanctioned as legitimate. Many Christians would have been quite content if Jesus' teaching on marriage had ended with his resounding reaffirmation of the Genesis ideal. Nonetheless, Matthew twice records Jesus' identification of the specific circumstances in which divorce remains permissible: 'except for marital unfaithfulness' (Mt 5:32; 19:9). Some have objected that the absence of this phrase in Mark and Luke must indicate that this clause was an addition by Matthew in order to authorise permission for strictly regulated divorce among the churches for whom he was writing. There is however no justification for relegating to the status of a clumsy editorial emendation a phrase that creates difficulty for some traditional church teaching.

The key word in Jesus' exceptive clause is *porneia*, for which the literal meaning is 'marital unfaithfulness'. Three interpretations have frequently been offered. First, some have suggested that in this context the word has the specific and narrow meaning of adultery. Jesus would therefore be unreservedly endorsing the approach of the school of Shammai. The case for *porneia* to mean adultery is certainly logically consistent with the rest of Jesus' argument. Since Jesus is arguing that sexual union within a subsequent unlawful marriage is adulterous, then an adulterous liaison within marriage can be nothing less than the definitive violation and repudiation of the marriage covenant. The adulterous sex act is not merely an act of intimate betrayal of the marriage partner, but actually establishes a new sexual union in place of the marriage union. Adultery, by definition, destroys marriage. The public act of divorce is then understood to be no more than the formal recognition that the marriage has already been brought to an end in the adulterous union. In Jewish thinking at the time of Jesus, such a divorce was an automatic and obligatory action for an aggrieved husband. According to this interpretation, the

additional clause in Matthew is not introducing new exceptions to the ideal of permanence, but is merely making
explicit what Jews at the time of Jesus took for granted.
Adultery destroys the marriage union, so a subsequent
divorce does no more than recognise that the marriage has
already been brought to an end.

Second, some have argued that *porneia* means a marriage
between close relatives, within the categories forbidden in
Leviticus 18:6–18. Some Gentiles allowed such marriages,
and the Jews tolerated them among Gentile converts to
Judaism. Such liaisons were likely therefore to become a
problem for the church as it advanced among the Gentiles.
On this interpretation, Jesus' defence of the sanctity of
marriage is absolute and unqualified: he is not permitting
divorce but rather excluding from the status of marriage all
illicit and incestuous unions. This is an ingenious interpretation that overcomes the evident embarrassment of some
Christians that in his teaching on marriage Jesus is more
liberal than some of his followers would want him to be.
However, this interpretation does seem to represent special
pleading, for such a definition is outside the natural meaning
of the word *porneia*.

Third, others have argued that we should not attempt to
explain away the natural meaning of *porneia*; that is, 'marital
unfaithfulness'. After all, Jesus has been speaking directly
about adultery and lust in the previous messianic intensification, so it would have been very easy to make an explicit
reference to adultery if that continued to be the sole focus of
Jesus' concerns. On this basis, Jesus is indeed providing an
exceptive clause that encompasses a range of sexual and
relational betrayals and irregularities both before and during
marriage. That is, while *porneia* undoubtedly includes the
specific categories of adultery and illicit marriage with a close
relative, Matthew has quite deliberately used a broader term
in Greek to express Jesus' meaning. This is undoubtedly the

natural interpretation of Matthew's Greek, which means that Jesus is rejecting both great rabbinical traditions, and his view is stricter than Hillel yet more liberal than Shammai. As ever, Jesus presents himself in typical fashion over against both the rabbis and Moses as the definitive interpreter of God's ideal for marriage, as originally revealed in Genesis 2.

Accepting this third interpretation to be correct, we can sum up the implications of Jesus' third example of a new righteousness. First, Jesus defends the ideal of the sanctity of marriage. Second, he rejects his contemporaries' casual approach to divorce and remarriage, arguing that such remarriages are by definition adulterous. Third, he repudiates the authority of the rabbinical tradition by an outright dismissal of both schools. Fourth, alongside his defence of the ideal, Jesus accepts that in a fallen world it is necessary to recognise that some marriages will inevitably fail, so he gives permission for divorce within specific constraints. Fifth, Jesus' argument is not against casual remarriage but against casual divorce. In any circumstances where divorce is legitimate, Jesus clearly takes it for granted that remarriage will be the likely consequence. Sixth, while conventional Jewish teaching made divorce compulsory on grounds of adultery, Jesus gave his followers a right rather than an obligation to divorce on grounds of marital unfaithfulness. That is, his disciples were given the freedom either to seek a divorce or to forgive their partner and continue with their marriage. Seventh, Jesus introduced a new and unfamiliar emphasis upon reciprocity and equality, by teaching that divorced men as well as divorced women were liable to enter adulterous second marriages.

In the Western world today, divorce has become increasingly normative. It is no longer seen as a tragedy, a last resort when all else has failed, but has increasingly become the first course of action as soon as a marriage faces any turbulence. The statistics for marriage breakdown are well known, with four in ten marriages ending in divorce. Fresh and disturbing evidence of the increasing prevalence of divorce was made public in October 1997, when Broken Rites, an organisation that seeks to help the divorced and separated partners of the clergy, made the astonishing claim that marriage breakdown among the Anglican clergy has now risen to the same disastrous levels as in the rest of society.

Although this unwelcome statistic may indicate that in practice the church is now shifting to embrace the casual attitude of the school of Hillel, the official line of many denominations remains closer to the school of Shammai. It is very strange that in this sole instance the church has actually chosen to be stricter than Jesus, especially when it has specialised in turning a blind eye to many of the other radical demands of the Sermon on the Mount. Expressions of anger that Jesus condemned have become socially acceptable, but grounds for divorce that Jesus deemed acceptable have been rejected.

We should also briefly identify some of the more extreme Christian assertions that have no real basis in the teaching of Jesus. Some claim that divorce is always wrong and should be illegal, but Jesus accepts that it will sometimes be the regrettable but inevitable consequence of marital unfaithfulness. Some suggest that divorce may be unavoidable but remarriage should never be allowed, but Jesus simply took it for granted that remarriage would follow from divorce, whether or not a particular divorce was justifiable. Some propose that those who have been divorced should return to their original partner and attempt to resume the marriage, even where one or the other has subsequently remarried. As a mandatory demand laid upon those who have been divorced, such an approach can only be described as tyrannous and irresponsible, cruel and absurd. Compulsory resumption of a former marriage is never suggested in the New Testament and is specifically excluded in the Old.

Jesus' messianic intensification of the Jewish understanding of marriage introduces an entirely original approach. Contrary to the casualness of Hillel, Jesus reasserts the ideal of the absolute sanctity of marriage, and he repudiates easy divorce. At the same time, contrary to the legalism of Shammai, Jesus is merciful and realistic in establishing legitimate grounds for divorce and remarriage that are wider than adultery and yet kept within clear boundaries. The reaction of Jesus' disciples to his teaching on marriage and divorce is instructive. When divorce was so readily available, at least for men, they were horrified by what they considered Jesus' extremely strict approach: 'If this is the situation between a husband and wife, it is better not to marry' (Mt 19:10).

While Jesus' exceptive clause was broader than the school of Shammai, his approach was much narrower than current practice, which followed the school of Hillel. To a society that tolerates casual divorce, and has come to consider marriage breakdown as inevitable, Jesus' approach will seem harsh and reactionary. But to a church that forbids divorce, or allows divorce but forbids remarriage, Jesus' approach will seem remarkably liberal.

8

Messianic Intensifications
(b) Oaths, Revenge and Enemies
Matthew 5:33–48

The second trio of intensifications further sharpens the contrast between normal standards of behaviour and the new righteousness to which Jesus calls his disciples. Jesus demands absolute verbal integrity, declares our instinctive quest for revenge to be obsolete, superseded by the principles of non-retaliation and voluntary servanthood, and decrees that his disciples' willingness to love must encompass even their enemies and persecutors. Jesus' dedication to the priority of self-giving love and to the practical outworking of higher righteousness is unequivocal and his fulfilment of his own teaching is exemplary. There is no dividing line between theory and practice: the ethics and the man are one.

From extravagant oaths to transparent integrity

Jesus combines two Old Testament phrases to summarise the prevailing attitude to oaths in the old way of holy living. There should be no oath-breaking (Lev 19:12), and in particular oaths made to the Lord should be considered absolutely binding (Num 30:2; Deut 23:21). The intention of the Law was to promote integrity by demanding that oaths be taken seriously. We see a similar tradition in modern courts of law. Although the charge of perjury will be laid against a witness who is proved to have lied in court, their testimony is preceded not merely with a warning about this law but with a positive declaration that their words will be entirely truthful. In a number of countries, including Britain, this avowal of truthfulness is of course habitually solemnised by swearing upon the Bible.

In order to arrive at his championing of unqualified integrity, Jesus' approach is deliberately combative. First he attacks the convention of taking oaths with religious connotations. We should not swear by heaven, which is God's throne, by earth, which is God's footstool, or by Jerusalem, which is the city of God's promised Messiah. Such grandiose oath-taking presumes to lend credibility to our own words, but is entirely inappropriate. Since heaven, earth and the holy city cannot be subject to our authority, the oaths are gratuitous and meaningless. More than that, such presumptuous, even pompous, phrases demean and dishonour God, reducing him to the role of a sidekick or lackey whose obligation is to lend his endorsement to our words. From Jesus' perspective, even if an individual is renowned for the absolute reliability of their words, such oath-taking should still be strenuously avoided.

A second kind of traditional oath-taking is non-religious, but Jesus does not allow it any greater measure of acceptability. He presents for consideration a typical example: 'I swear by my head.' The equivalent English idiom would be: 'I swear by the very hairs of my head.' Without hesitation, Jesus mocks such oaths: we cannot turn a single hair white or black. In other words, even when we base oaths upon our own body, abilities or attributes, we are seeking to lend weight and credibility to our words through things over which we simply do not have control. Non-religious oaths are therefore equally gratuitous and meaningless since the truth or falsehood of our words will have no impact whatsoever upon the thing we have invoked to strengthen our credibility. Such claims are powerless and empty, so our oaths are cheap because they are ultimately and entirely inconsequential.

Oath-taking is a more or less universal human custom, so we can readily identify the dynamics of oath usage and the likely life cycle and evolution of oaths within a particular culture. When people want to emphasise that a particular statement is genuine and authoritative, an oath is often added to their words by way of reinforcement. However, the custom of habitual oath-taking tends to result in the devaluation of oaths, and so they become a casual part of everyday speech rather than being reserved for statements of great importance or definitive reliability. As the currency of oath-taking becomes debased, more exotic and extravagant phrases have to be employed to reinforce any really important declarations. A society that has been obliged to construct elaborate oaths in order for an assertion to be taken seriously has decayed to the point where integrity has been replaced by habitual lying. Eventually, in a period of decadence in oath-taking, a baroque encrustation of convoluted and extreme oaths comes to be attached to the words of renowned rogues. The more fulsome the oaths, the less likely it becomes that the words have any basis in truth and reliability. Extravagant oath-takers do indeed, in Shakespeare's phrase, 'protest too much'.

The Law came to the defence of integrity by demanding that we keep our oaths. Jesus' intention is exactly the same, for he too wants our words to become utterly reliable. However, Jesus' way of intensifying the Law is to propose a better way of achieving the same end. His higher righteousness is intended to persuade us that oaths are worthless and should be avoided. More than that, Jesus requires such consummate integrity that he raises the possibility of never needing to take an oath at all. In the new righteousness, he calls his disciples to an absolute transparency, a crystalline integrity, in which their 'yes' and 'no' will require no additional emphatic phrases or avowals to be found convincing and trustworthy. There should be no credibility gap, however small, between truth and our witness; between our promises and their fulfilment.

We must inevitably consider the implications of Jesus' comprehensive exclusion of oaths for the taking of oaths in a modern court. In Jesus' own trial, the high priest sought to impose a solemn oath upon Jesus: 'I charge you under oath by the living God: Tell us if you are the Christ, the Son of God' (Mt 26:63). Jesus did not have the luxury of being able to decline to accept the terms of this charge – there was no freedom of conscience faced with the court of the Sanhedrin. In his response Jesus declined to make the oath 'I do solemnly swear, by the living God . . . ' his own. Rather, in line with his own teaching, Jesus' reply begins with the directness of a simple affirmative: 'Yes, it is as you say' (Mt 26:64).

There are, however, occasional statements within the New Testament which may be interpreted as oaths: 'I call God as my witness' (2 Cor 1:23); 'I assure you before God that what I am writing to you is no lie' (Gal 1:20); 'I charge you before the Lord to have this letter read' (1 Thess 5:27). Even if these phrases are not oaths in the strict sense, they do at least indicate a grey area of forceful expression when emphatic language comes close to oath-taking. In Hebrews 6:13–17, God is described as taking an oath in his own name, but this is metaphorical language designed to convey the principle that God's promises are utterly binding, both on earth and in heaven.

Our response to the question of oaths in court must identify two equal and opposite errors. If we become obsessed with the details of outward conformity we miss out on the heart of the messianic intensifications, reverting to the legalistic mentality of the Pharisees. On the other hand, if we fit in with our society uncritically, hastily explaining away every uncomfortable demand, we will quickly lose sight of the heightened radicalism of Jesus' call to a new righteousness. In my own view, the natural interpretation of Jesus' words prompts us to decline to swear on the Bible, but the priority of grace should mean that we are careful to avoid obsessiveness or judgementalism faced with other believers who interpret Jesus' demands differently.

Above all, while we are bound to consider the implications of Jesus' teaching for the specific demands of a modern law court, we should be careful not to lose sight of the universal implications which are uppermost in this particular intensification of the Law. Jesus invites his disciples to attain such renown for absolute trustworthiness that any suggestion that we should be made to take an oath will be considered entirely superfluous. Jesus is not simply against oath-taking. He is seeking to promote the very highest standards of personal integrity. Irrespective of the standards of honesty in the surrounding culture, the word of true disciples should always be their bond.

From revenge to willing service

In modern usage 'an eye for an eye, a tooth for a tooth' has reversed its ancient meaning. For us, it suggests exacting the full measure of revenge, a remorseless pursuit of all that is our due. However, among the ancient Hebrews this was understood to be a restrictive law, limiting the scope of revenge and retaliation by setting an unambiguous upper limit. Every few years the newspapers are filled with lurid stories of gangland killings, with rival gangs exacting revenge in an ever-increasing spiral of violence, each seeking to outdo the brutal excesses of their opponents. In a society where families were only too ready to take the law into their own hands, the threefold repetition in the Old Testament of the *lex talionis* was designed to exclude an escalating cycle of revenge attacks (Exod 21:24; Deut 19:21; Lev 24:20). By the time of Jesus, physical retribution had been replaced by financial compensation. In the fifth of his messianic intensifications, Jesus therefore does not focus upon violent and bloody retaliation, but explores the much wider issue of how to respond to those who do us harm.

Jesus introduces his higher righteousness by proposing a general principle that is quite shocking: 'Do not resist an evil person' (Mt 5:39). Although this verb could be used of taking someone to court, the meaning is broader, excluding any kind of resistance at all. In order to intensify the Law, Jesus does not merely invite us to leave aside retaliation and revenge. It is not merely violence, but all resistance that Jesus' words preclude. This messianic extremism of non-retaliatory servanthood is, of course, precisely fulfilled by Jesus during his arrest and trial, scourging and crucifixion.

Jesus explores the priorities of mercy rather than revenge and of radical servanthood rather than self-assertion through four vivid and memorable mini-parables. In the first, someone is struck upon the right cheek. This indicates that they have been slapped with the back of the right hand, which signified in the ancient world not a full-blooded blow but a violent gesture of contempt, for which a court would heavily fine the assailant. The setting, therefore, is one of violent mockery rather than an all-out physical assault. The instinctive response to such provocation would be to hit back; a calmer victim would take their attacker to court. Jesus does not merely reject the violent response, but he invites his disciples to forego their legal rights. To turn the other cheek is not an act of defiance – 'Hit me if you dare!' – but rather an act of absurdity, a calculated renunciation of our rights. This response is exemplified by Jesus' absolute

non-resistance to the attacks that accompanied his trial,
when he was both struck and slapped (Mt 26:67). Implicit
in this first mini-parable may therefore be the specific experience of contemptuous assault during a time of persecution.
The Servant Songs of Isaiah anticipate this extraordinary and
absolute refusal to retaliate: 'I offered my back to those who
beat me, my cheeks to those who pulled out my beard; I did
not hide my face from mocking and spitting' (Is 50:6).

In the second mini-parable, someone sues a believer and
lays claim to his tunic. In Jewish Law, the outer garment
could never be confiscated through the courts. For human-
itarian reasons, everyone was entitled to be left with the
cloak on their back (Exod 22:25–27). Once again, Jesus'
intensification is extreme: the zeal of the litigant should be
surpassed by the zeal of the Christian victim, who should
willingly hand over his cloak as a bonus alongside the tunic.

In the third mini-parable, a Roman soldier had the right
to require an imperial subject to serve as his beast of burden
for a mile. This regulation was enforced when Simon of
Cyrene was made to carry Jesus' cross. There could be no
compulsion to enjoy the experience of serving as forced
labour, and no doubt most people fulfilled this task reluctantly, even begrudgingly, if they dared to show dissent.
Jesus once more violates the canons of common sense by
proposing that the disciple volunteer to carry the load for a
second mile. Once again there is no implication of defiance,
no suggesting that the imperial soldier will see the error of
his ways as a result of such willing service. The disciple is
called to serve in direct contradiction to our instinctive self-
assertion or desire for revenge.

In the fourth mini-parable, someone seeks to borrow
money. The believer is told not to turn the person away,
but to give or lend willingly and generously in response to
another's needs.

Taken together, these four mini-parables demonstrate a

brilliant and penetrating insight into ways in which we become defensive and protective of our own rights. Under physical assault, we want to fight back or go to law. If our possessions are under threat, we want to defend ourselves, keeping all that we can. If a foreign soldier imposes tyrannous obligations, we want to do as little as possible, dragging our feet as we reluctantly comply with his demands. If someone asks to borrow money, our instinct is to refer them to a bank or wonder whether they will really be able to repay us. These parables therefore have a much wider impact than the specific issue of revenge and non-retaliation. They explore a new resolve not to stand up for our own rights but to serve others willingly. Mother Teresa summed up this messianic intensification in a memorable phrase: to 'love until it hurts'. Such a life of service is nothing less than absurd. And yet it is the way of Jesus.

Luke's complementary passage reveals further dimensions of Jesus' extremism. Here the physical assault is aggressive rather than a backhanded slap on the right cheek; the cloak is taken by violent theft, and the disciple is to do nothing to defend himself against his tunic being similarly stolen; the one who asks is probably a beggar rather than a borrower; and we should not demand the return of items others have taken – whether with or without our permission (Lk 6:29–31).

We have deliberately delayed addressing some of the questions begged by this teaching. If we turn too quickly to consider ways in which this intensification does not apply, there is great danger that we might lose its force altogether and evade its extreme demands. Some have argued that these verses make the case for non-violent resistance. Certainly Jesus was Martin Luther King's inspiration when he espoused non-violence in the Civil Rights movement. Nonetheless, while non-violent resistance is an honourable deduction from the lifestyle of Jesus, in this particular section of the Great Sermon, Jesus emphasises a complete lack of resistance to evil, whether physically or through a court of law.

Others see in these verses a basis for Christian pacifism. Once again, we must acknowledge that no case can be made more powerfully for Christian pacifism than the lifestyle of Jesus. However, although the opening principle of this section emphasises a general principle of non-resistance, the four mini-parables all specifically concern attacks upon the individual. Jesus simply does not address in this section of the Great Sermon legitimate ways in which to come to the defence of others. Similarly, since Jesus' illustrations all quite deliberately concern individuals, it would be simplistic and unjustified to transfer this teaching directly to the role of the state, whether in terms of a police force and penal system or in terms of maintaining a standing army and being prepared to go to war. These are complex issues, in which the radical anabaptist and pacifist positions, which strongly argue against Christian participation in the judicial system and the military, should certainly not be ignored within the Christian debate. But theirs is a minority voice, and the vast majority of Christians would accept that in certain circumstances it is legitimate and necessary to have recourse to a controlled measure of violence in defence of the powerless against their assailants – not only as compassionate individuals, but also when a nation reluctantly goes to war against an aggressor or sends a peace-keeping force overseas.

Perhaps more than any other of the messianic intensifications, the great danger with the fifth is that while a few may attempt a naive and literal fulfilment of the illustrative mini-parables, the majority may dismiss the whole notion as impossible and unrealistic. Jesus' language is deliberately extreme, using vivid mini-parables to demonstrate the strength of our instinctive retaliatory responses. His concern is not that we should slavishly put into practice the mini-parables which make his case with calculated hyperbole. If we did, Christians would be easily recognisable: bruised on both cheeks, naked, strong in the legs and shoulders through regular voluntary service as porters, and completely impoverished, having surrendered all our money indiscriminately to passing beggars.

Jesus' arresting examples do not add up to a new law code. They could not possibly, since Jesus is not providing an exhaustive set of precedents but rather is seeking to establish an attitude of radical servanthood, even towards opponents in law and occupying forces, muggers and beggars. The fifth intensification demands not merely non-retaliation but an active willingness to serve even our most unjust and exploitative assailants. We need to embrace the spirit of this intensification, not the letter of the mini-parables. One has already done so supremely, for he showed nothing of retaliation, self-defence and self-vindication during his arrest, trial and crucifixion. He did not merely eschew revenge, he served to the uttermost. And to a similar extremism of servanthood he has unambiguously called his followers.

From loving neighbours to loving enemies

In his sixth and final intensification, Jesus quotes once again from the Mosaic Law: 'Love your neighbour' (Lev 19:18), together with its corollary: 'and hate your enemy'. The second half of Jesus' quotation cannot be found in the Jewish scriptures, and it redefines the second love command in terms that are sectarian and exclusive. Jesus flatly contradicts this approach. Rather than simply reaffirming that love of neighbours is universally applicable, Jesus expressly insists that his disciples should love their enemies. This has nothing to do with an emotional response but is expressed in generous actions. Jesus clarifies this love in two distinct ways: we should pray for them (Mt 5:44) and we should do them good (Lk 6:35). In the Jewish context, 'neighbours' would indicate fellow Jews and the 'enemies' would be hostile Gentiles. Jesus repositions the neighbour and enemy dualism in terms of brothers – that is, fellow Christians (Mt 5:47) – and persecutors (Mt 5:44).

The disciples' responsibility to love their enemies is emphasised through two comparisons. First, Jesus explains that to love our enemies will make us truly sons of the Father, expressing the family likeness in self-giving love. Jesus illustrates the Father's love in terms of the equal availability of the sun and rain to the entire human race. This may appear to suggest that the Father's love is indiscriminate, but Jesus' use of two pairs of contrasting descriptions – 'evil and good', 'righteous and unrighteous' – indicates that the Father's love is clear-sighted and yet inclusive: the secrets of our character can never be hidden from the Father's gaze and yet he still chooses to express his love to the entire human race. Even so, we must learn to be inclusive in our love.

Second, Jesus compares his disciples' love with that of tax collectors and pagans. Both groups were despised by many Jews – the pagans because they neither worshipped God nor obeyed his law; the tax collectors because they were collaborators with the Roman Empire and exploiters of those from whom they collected taxes. Many Jews would have considered both to be inferior types of human being. Jesus therefore provokes a common prejudice among his hearers to bring home the fact that it is perfectly normal for men and women to love those who love them and greet those who greet them. There is nothing impressive or generous about such love, no room for self-congratulation. Normal human love operates in such a way, within the boundaries of exclusive cliques. What Jesus demands is nothing less than inclusive love. His intensification of the Pharisaical way of righteousness is designed to produce a group of disciples who do not merely abstain from hatred, but are known for their active love even for their persecutors, praying for them and doing them good.

As soon as Jesus completes his sixth example of a messianic intensification he provides a final, summary principle. This section began with a remarkable challenge, explaining that our righteousness must exceed that of the Pharisees (Mt 5:20). The concluding climax captures the essence of this new and higher righteousness: 'Be perfect, therefore, as your heavenly Father is perfect' (Mt 5:48). This is an echo of the summary command of the Mosaic Law: 'Be holy because I, the Lord your God, am holy' (Lev 19:2).

The very concept of holiness had been tarnished by the legalistic negativity of the Pharisees. According to Jesus' intensifications of the Law, his followers should not be known primarily as 'the people who don't', but rather as 'the people who love'. The extravagant, inclusive love of the Father should find practical expression in the lifestyle of true discipleship. The perfection of the Father that we are called to emulate cannot be found in the divine power and attributes – his eternal nature, omniscience, omnipotence and omnipresence. Such qualities are beyond all emulation by the human race. But the character of God – supremely manifest in Jesus himself, who not merely taught but lived his messianic intensifications of the Law, fulfilling the Law in his daily living – this is the perfection to which we are called. Jesus therefore points us not only towards moral purity, but also to wholeness, just as his own life was perfectly integrated and complete. The call to perfection is a call to purity, integrity and wholeness in every relationship – in mind and heart, at work and at home – in wholehearted imitation of Christ.

Once again we must note the double impact of Jesus' teaching. On the one hand the call to perfection is a counsel of despair. If perfection is the minimum requirement of the Father and the Son, who can hope to be saved? Jesus' teaching therefore points to the necessity of his atoning death and the need for saving faith and imputed righteousness. To be perfect, it is essential that by faith in Christ we become 'clothed in righteousness divine'. At the same time, for those who have come to faith, there can be no room for complacency. Jesus' words are designed to quicken high aspirations, not just in the first flush of young faith, but in a lifelong pursuit of growth in discipleship. The perfection of the Father, manifest in the life of the Son, inspires and beckons us to continued advance in self-giving love and purity of heart.

As the messianic intensifications reach their climax, the degree to which Jesus calls his followers to a righteousness beyond the Pharisees becomes ever more apparent. Quite unlike the external conformity at which the Pharisees excelled, the ways of Jesus are beyond legislation or compulsion. Every moment in which we seek to live by this new righteousness, we take a fresh risk of faith. Common sense and self-interest make uncomfortable neighbours to the alternative lifestyle of Jesus. Just like the eighth and final beatitude, the last of the messianic intensifications acknowledges the practical inevitability of persecution. The shadow of the cross falls once again across the Great Sermon. The way of perfection proves also to be the way of persecution.

There is a particularly striking correlation between this second trio of intensifications and Jesus' last days in Jerusalem. When he is put on trial, although he is placed under an enforced oath by the authorities, Jesus' few words in his own defence have an unvarnished simplicity and directness. When he is mocked and struck by the soldiers, he offers no retaliation, just as at the time of his arrest in Gethsemane Peter's attempt to defend him with a sword was totally repudiated. Even as he suffers the excruciating agony of crucifixion, his only words for his persecutors are a remarkably generous prayer of appeal for the Father to forgive them. Matthew must have recognised this astonishingly detailed parallelism between the passion of Christ and the last three messianic intensifications. Jesus not only lived by the Sermon on the Mount, he died by it.

PART THREE

The Way of Freedom
Matthew 6

9

Freedom from Human Religion –
True and Hidden Spirituality
Matthew 6:1–6, 16–18

Although Christianity has long since taken its place as one of
the great world religions (indeed the largest and most influ-
ential), much of the characteristic style and many of the
predominant values of the Christian religion have little to
do with the teaching of Jesus. So far out of step was Jesus
with conventional religion that he was often in trouble with
the Pharisees precisely for not being religious enough. The
pomp and ceremony, the love and abuse of power, the sheer
religiosity all demonstrate that Christianity has characteristi-
cally proved to be a complex combination of human religion
and the spiritual revolution of the preacher from Galilee.

Having presented the way of fulfilment explored in the
Beatitudes, and then the way of perfection explored in
the messianic intensifications, in Matthew 6 Jesus turns
to the way of freedom. The breaking of prisoners' chains was
integral to the messianic hope of the Old Testament: 'The
Spirit of the Sovereign LORD is on me, because the LORD has
anointed me to preach good news to the poor. He has sent
me to bind up the broken-hearted, to proclaim freedom for
the captives and release from darkness for the prisoners' (Is
61:1); 'As for you, because of the blood of my covenant with
you, I will free your prisoners from the waterless pit. Return

to your fortress, O prisoners of hope; even now I announce that I will restore twice as much to you' (Zech 9:11–12). Jesus not only used Isaiah 61 to launch and describe his public ministry (Lk 4:16–21), he also gave an explicit invitation to discover and receive personal liberation, offering to his followers a freedom that could not be taken away, and life in all its fullness: 'So if the Son sets you free, you will be free indeed' (Jn 8:36); 'The thief comes only to steal and kill and destroy; I have come that they may have life, and have it to the full' (Jn 10:10). Peter summed up the disciples' conviction that Jesus was their spiritual liberator: 'Lord, to whom shall we go? You have the words of eternal life' (Jn 6:68).

Since the sixties, the West has worked on the assumption that freedom and fulfilment arise from 'doing your own thing'. We have overthrown universal moral frameworks, suggesting that they crush the spirit of the individual. The consensus is that we need to invent our own, personal morality. Society tells us, 'You can believe whatever you like, so long as just two conditions are met: you don't cause injury to anyone else (other than babies in the womb), and you don't try to impose your beliefs on anyone else.' The only absolute truth is that there are no absolute truths. The only moral absolute is that we cannot encroach on one another's moral liberty. This dominant approach of our era is both illogical and unworkable. Illogical, because the statements that exclude absolutes make absolutist claims for themselves. Unworkable, because in practice certain patterns of behaviour are still deemed completely unacceptable, and rightly so. More than that, many non-Christian politicians, journalists and opinion-formers are beginning to express growing concern that we have established a society in which children are increasingly finding it difficult to know right from wrong.

When everyone does their own thing, the result is not

liberation for all but licence for the powerful. A society that sinks into moral decadence sees the rich able to indulge every whim while turning a blind eye to the plight of the poor. The great myth of our age is that the repudiation of moral absolutes leads to personal freedom and fulfilment. Look at Hollywood, a world of remarkable wealth and privilege, where indulgence comes easy but relationships are brittle, where the sincerity often seems as plastic as the surgery. Jesus' diagnosis is that true freedom comes to those who choose to follow him because genuine fulfilment is found in a life of service. He identifies three crucial kinds of enslavement from which he offers to set us free: religious bondage, materialistic captivity and the encircling chains of anxiety.

Establishing the contrast

Just as folk tales often use a rule of three – three sisters, three wishes, three princes – Jesus' teaching frequently uses the same pattern – three servants given loans, three excuses for not coming to the banquet, three passers-by on the road from Jerusalem to Jericho, and so on. The rule of three provides a familiar structure that draws in his hearers, who then await some kind of surprise or key point in the punch-line. It also provides the necessary framework for popular preaching in a pre-literate society. The predictable structure is easy to remember, and so the teaching can be passed on reliably by word of mouth.

In Matthew 6, the essential pattern is established in the opening warning: 'Be careful not to do your "acts of right-eousness" before men, to be seen by them. If you do, you will have no reward from your Father in heaven' (v.1). The note of warning is immediately sounded: *be careful in public*. The general theme is established: *righteous acts*. The pro-blem motivation is pinpointed: *to be seen and approved by men*. And the resultant judgement is spelled out: *no reward from the Father*. In what follows, Jesus elaborates this principle three times, with reference to giving, praying and fasting. Jesus' primary emphasis is not to commend these acts of devotion – since he is speaking to Jews he takes it for granted that they will continue to practise these spiritual disciplines. The key principle is hiddenness: doing them in the sight of God alone.

Watchdog, the leading British TV programme on consumer affairs, had a long-running item concerning Ford Mondeos. The steering had a habit of developing a will of its own, causing the car to be reluctant to travel in a straight line, preferring to veer off gradually towards the side of the road. Ford have now announced that the problem only affected a minority of cars and the cause has long since been eradicated. In the opening words of Matthew 6, Jesus is warning us against a kind of 'Ford Mondeo' spirituality, a built-in tendency to veer away from the hiddenness that Jesus commends. It seems that our natural instinct is to perform religious duties as a public display in order to win the praise and admiration of men and women. If we did not have such a strong bias towards outward religiosity, Jesus would not have bothered to give such a clear, vigorous and sustained warning. In his threefold instruction, Jesus invites us to go against the grain, to break the mould, to refuse to conform to the usual pattern of human religion.

The repeated pattern is made more complex and obscure in the middle section, because when Jesus teaches on prayer he chooses to cover three more themes: praying like the Gentiles, the Lord's Prayer, and the connection between prayer and forgiveness. For the moment, we shall leave this additional trio to one side, concentrating on the three-fold instruction that follows the pattern of the introduction. *When* you perform a certain task, *do not* be like the hypocrites, who seek human appreciation (6:2, 5, 16). Instead, do it in a *hidden way*, so that your Father, who sees in secret, will reward you (6:3–4, 6, 17–18).

Empty displays

The wrong approach to each type of religious duty is illustrated in a mini-parable, all three being drawn from familiar experiences in first-century Palestine. When it came to giving, some of the wealthy in Jesus' day announced their offering by hiring a trumpeter. His job was to herald their generosity on street corners and in the temple. Such a literal parade of human kindness seems preposterous and vulgar today. How could anyone be so self-centred and arrogant that even their giving became another pretext for self-aggrandisement and self-adulation?

While trumpeters have gone out of fashion, we have found other ways of making a public spectacle of our kindness. During TV-sponsored charity fundraising events, it has become customary to emblazon the names of donors across the foot of the screen. Others gather in the studio clutching outsize cheques waiting to announce their donation on camera and so obtain their thirty seconds of personal fame and public approval. A century ago, the same desire for public display found expression through newspaper reports that listed the subscribers to particular charitable schemes. Like most excesses of the Victorian era such self-serving displays did not escape the scourge of Dickens' pen, notably in Mrs Jellyby and Mrs Pardiggle in *Bleak House*. Mrs Jellyby was so devoted to Africa that her children were constantly neglected. Mrs Pardiggle's proud boast was that her children's names could often be seen in public subscription lists, for she had persuaded them 'voluntarily' to give extensively to charity: 'My young family are not frivolous; they expend the entire amount of their allowance on subscriptions, under my direction . . .'

As to praying, Jesus condemns standing in the synagogue and on street corners. It's not the posture to which Jesus objects. Nor is it really the location, since a synagogue and a street corner are perfectly reasonable places to pray. It is the motivation behind the praying for which Jesus has no time. His world was littered with people who, though they never spoke a word to God in private, found a sudden desire to pray eloquently whenever other people could see them. On the street corners their prayers were ostentatious, an elaborate and unmissable public spirituality that declared unmistakably to passers-by how very religious and devoted they were. The synagogue had degenerated into a place where such people went not to meet with God but to be seen by men. Jesus sweeps aside such empty showiness as a blight upon true religion. I regret to have to acknowledge that I have sometimes met people who pray eloquently in public but never pray in private; people whose lives show little or nothing of living discipleship who make a great display of going to church on Sundays; people whose spirituality is all show and no substance. Jesus' warnings have by no means passed their sell-by date.

In a related parable, Jesus contrasted the approaches to prayer of a Pharisee and a tax collector (Lk 18:10–14). The Pharisee was righteous in his own eyes, and proudly listed his accomplishments before God – fasting twice a week and tithing rigorously. But even as he preened himself, making complacent comparisons with the tax collector, the truth was that God was nowhere near the centre of his attention. He was so full of himself that even though he notionally addressed his thoughts to God he was really only speaking for his own, self-congratulatory benefit. His devotion might win him human admiration, but God saw straight through his arrogance and self-obsession. According to Jesus the way to being right with God is found not when we list our accomplishments, but when we discover the need to pray humbly for divine mercy. The prayer that Jesus commended was appropriate not just for one particular tax collector, but for all who aspire to be true disciples: 'God, have mercy on me, a sinner' (Lk 18:13).

Jesus' third example of religious display takes most of us into more unfamiliar territory. While giving and prayer remain almost universal Christian practices, fasting is a much more endangered species of spiritual discipline. Ironically, one particular kind of fasting is more popular than ever before; that is, dieting. However, dieting has two distinctive and regrettable characteristics: it is fasting without reference to God, and for most people it usually ends in failure! Still more unfamiliar than the practice of fasting is the kind of accompanying public display that was familiar to Jesus' contemporaries. Jesus' parable about self-righteous praying indicates that the custom of some Jews was not to fast on rare occasions and in extreme circumstances, but rather to fast twice every week. Some Jews concluded that it was hardly worth enduring this regular and almost obligatory fasting without making sure that others knew about it. They therefore made a public display of their devoted endurance, disfiguring their faces with a pained expression, having dishevelled hair or even rubbing ashes into their skin.

The modern equivalents are less ostentatious, but equally lacking in subtlety: those who cannot miss a meal without letting others know about it, or those who join others for lunch or dinner, only to declare that they won't be eating anything because they are fasting. According to Jesus, such a performance may win the approval or admiration of others, but God is not fooled or impressed. Putting on a show means that a fast becomes worthless in God's eyes, no matter how over-awed men and women may be by what seems to be conclusive evidence of our saintly dedication.

The lust for recognition

Jesus' description of anyone who indulges these three forms of behaviour is uncompromising: they are *hypocrites*. His intolerance arises because spiritual disciplines should be directed only towards God, in love and in humble submission. Such motivation completely excludes any pursuit of self-promotion, but that is exactly what is being pursued in the super-spiritual antics that Jesus condemns. In Jesus' three mini-parables we see people with one eye always on the main chance, desperate to be noticed and admired for their religious dedication.

What causes religious activities to degenerate to such a degree? Deep human instincts of self-interest find expression in the need to be noticed, the hunger for appreciation and the lust for status – whether social, political or religious. These competitive and self-assertive drives can be harnessed and redirected for the good, but if they are untamed they can dominate our inner life. They become terrible taskmasters, producing people who are driven, restless and miserable, even in their moments of greatest success.

Just as Jesus criticised the Pharisees for their showy displays of pretended religious devotion, we need to acknowledge that these instincts were not exterminated with the birth of the church. On the contrary, church history is littered with examples of similar excesses. The cult of self-promotion can all too easily be carried over into the life of the church, contaminating or even uprooting the inner purity and outward simplicity commended by Jesus. Spectacular outward displays of religious devotion can conceal an inner vacuum in the secret spaces of the spirit. No Christian denomination, stream or tradition is exempt. From formal pomp to fiery preacher, from robed priest to robust prophet, all can be tempted by the self-congratulatory power games of putting on an impressive religious show. Shakespeare's words sum up the real value of such religious flummery: 'full of sound and fury, signifying nothing' (*Macbeth*, Act 5, scene 5).

Jesus' blunt condemnation gives us no permission to shoot from the hip in sweeping and sudden disparagement of any Christians of whom we disapprove. Rather, Jesus' severity puts each one of us in the divine spotlight. Time and again we need to ask of ourselves the same question: Is it possible that I have begun to drift from my moorings in Jesus' new way of living, moving instead with the natural flow of the tide of human religion?

Not only does such parading of imaginary devotion receive Jesus' present condemnation, these religious performers have nothing to look forward to from the Father. Their performance is inflated, the object of devotion is not God but self, and the approval that has been pursued, and even secured, is human not divine. For all their efforts, the devotees of human religion have been dedicated to activities that are ultimately pointless. Three times Jesus sums up their fate, the repetition beating out a stark warning of the futility of human religion: 'they have received their reward in full' (6:2, 5, 16). Those whose eyes have been fixed on human approval should expect no favours from God. Our Father in heaven is neither fooled nor impressed by a self-serving religious performance.

Hidden spirituality

As Jesus explores the abuses of religion as a public display, he identifies three distinctive facets of authentic spirituality.

1. *True spirituality needs to discover the virtue of maximum hiddenness.* Jesus uses a psychological impossibility to express the crucial importance of secrecy. It's as if the left hand asks: 'How much have you given in the offering today?' To which the right hand promptly replies: 'It's

confidential! There's absolutely no way I'm going to tell you!'

2. *True spirituality should have unseen depths*. The most important place in which to pray is behind closed doors, seen only by the Father.

3. *True spirituality should actively conceal rather than make a parade of the cost of devotion*. Whereas hypocrites go to the ridiculous extreme of disfiguring their faces when fasting, the true disciple will not merely avoid grumbling about hunger pangs, but will make a point of maintaining a well-groomed appearance.

Two key words punctuate this threefold repetition. Twice the Father is described as 'unseen' (6:6, 18); four times the approved spirituality is 'in secret' (6:4 twice, 6, 18). Here is a new kind of walk with God – a hidden, inward spirituality with completely different priorities from the public displays of human religion. For the true disciple, the desire to please the heavenly Father in secret is intended to become not merely something we try to bear in mind, but our governing priority.

If we embraced Jesus' single-mindedness, his approach would release the true disciple from the disastrous bondage of keeping up with religious appearances. When the sole and focused motivation of true spirituality is to please the Father in secret, we can afford to become indifferent to any criticism of our unconventionality from those who prefer ostentatious displays of public religiosity. Jesus also explains that hiddenness is the route to blessedness. Just as those whose spirituality is self-serving receive their full reward from the men and women they are trying to please or impress, the Father sees clearly what is done in secret and this is the authentic spirituality that wins his favour. Jesus declines to spell out the nature of that reward, preferring to emphasise that the Father's approval comes not to outward religious conformity but to the hidden devotion of the inner life.[1]

Jesus' examples of true spirituality are typically extreme. In practice we might protest, 'How can I possibly keep my left and right hand from knowing what has been given to the needy?' There is both a personal and a corporate application here. As individuals, we benefit from cultivating an attitude of absent-mindedness. Once money has been handed over, we need to eradicate every possibility of enduring self-congratulation for our generosity.

Within local churches, we need to protect everyone from unhealthy responses when someone makes a large gift, and that is best done by managing church finances within a framework of confidentiality that is absolutely watertight. I have come across leadership teams who are terrified of doing anything that their 'big giver' might not like for fear of catastrophic consequences for the church budget. This can happen even when the individual concerned would have no desire to hold a gun to the heads of the church leaders through their generous giving. Such problems arise when too many people have come to know too many financial details. Of course, if money is offered with strings attached (I heard of one North American church where a man offered 'personal financial support' to a minister so long as he could join the church board) the gift should be returned. On one occasion I came across a church where a major donor to a building project was allowed to see the accounts, simply because no one liked to turn down his request. Once he discovered how large a proportion of the giving came from his own pocket, it undermined his attitude to the church. Jesus' principle of secrecy is built upon a profound pastoral insight: widespread knowledge about who gives what in a local church can destroy the good intentions that may have originally been the sole motivation for our giving.

Jesus' other examples require less explanation. He cannot be suggesting that the only proper place to pray is in splendid isolation behind closed doors, since we know of many occasions when he prayed in the company of others. Instead, Jesus is surely indicating that public prayer needs to become the tip of an iceberg. When we pray in public we need not only to ensure that our prayers are intended to please God rather than impress men and women, we also need to ensure a healthy sense of proportion between public and private praying.

Likewise, Jesus' concern that we should conceal private fasting behind a healthy appearance does not mean that a general call in a church, denomination or nation to a period of fasting is categorically outlawed. Rather, Jesus is warning us that our acts of piety will be entirely nullified if we give in to the temptation to win the approval or admiration of our fellow believers through our spiritual exploits. Just as most of an iceberg lies beneath the waves, Jesus commends a spirituality with hidden depths, seen and known only by our Father in heaven. Here is the essence of true spirituality: it is for God's eyes only.

10

Freedom in Prayer
Matthew 6:7–15

There is a story from the Second World War of some Londoners huddled in an air raid shelter during a bombing raid. The exploding bombs were deafening, terrifying and dangerously close. Someone suggested that it would be a good idea to pray, but none of the adults was willing to take the lead, not really knowing how to express their needs and fears in the form of a prayer. A young boy came to their rescue by volunteering eagerly. Silence fell in the air raid shelter as everyone bowed their heads and waited for their 'priest of the moment' to take the lead. Drawing himself up to full height he prayed the only prayer he knew: 'For what we are about to receive, may the Lord make us truly thankful.'

We saw in the last chapter that the threefold structure of Jesus' development of the theme of hidden or inner spirituality was interrupted by a threefold exploration of further aspects of prayer: the abuses of the Gentiles, the Lord's Prayer, and the importance of forgiveness. It seems that Jesus recognised how easily our praying can be trapped within a shallow conformity to a rigid and superficial set of human rules about how to pray properly. Once again his words provide a spiritual liberation as he introduces a new kind of directness and simplicity into the life of prayer.

164

The babbling of pagans

If the Jews' great temptation was to seek to win the approval or admiration of others through praying in public places in ways that could not be missed, Jesus thought that the Gentiles made a religious virtue out of foolish and idle repetition. To the civilised peoples of the Roman Empire, it seemed that the Barbarians living beyond the borders did little but babble. The very name 'Barbarians' was coined to echo the inchoate, unintelligible speech of those primitives who had failed to learn Greek or Latin, the common languages of the many peoples of the Imperial World. It was as if they were constantly repeating a single, meaningless syllable: 'Bar, bar, bar.' Jesus is concerned to dispose of the tendency to pile up words in pointless repetition as if the use of many phrases guarantees a good and effective prayer that will be answered promptly. He describes the practice as 'babbling like the pagans', and he sums up the intention with 'They think they will be heard because of their many words' (6:7).

To his Jewish audience, Jesus' words may well have recalled the classic Old Testament account of futile praying, when the Baalite priests unwisely entered into a spiritual competition with Elijah at Mount Carmel (1 Kings 18:26–29). From morning till noon they kept up their repetition, shouting out their appeal: 'Oh Baal, answer us!' When the skies stayed silent, they took to shouting even louder and then began to slash themselves with swords and spears. As the blood flowed they worked themselves into a frenzy, prophesying with a frantic intensity. Clearly they gave everything they could to the task of securing a response from Baal. Their desperate, ecstatic antics continued until the time of the evening sacrifice, but with no success. Elijah mocked them mercilessly: 'Perhaps he is deep in thought, or busy, or travelling. Maybe he is sleeping and must be awakened.' Finally the compiler of this history of ancient Israel sums up the futility of their efforts: 'But there was no response, no-one answered, no-one paid attention' (v.29).

Two errors characterise this over-strenuous approach to prayer. First there is an obsession with technique. The underlying assumption is that if we can only find the right way of praying – the right words, the right volume or even the right kind of self-mutilating frenzy – then the success of our prayers will be guaranteed at last. Second, there is an obsession with effort. Here the underlying assumption is that the results are ultimately up to us. The sovereign will of God is entirely replaced by human responsibility, as we attempt to badger and hound the Almighty into complying with our demands.

It would be entirely unrealistic to suppose that these errors died with the Baalite priests of Elijah's day or the pagans of the time of Jesus. Throughout the centuries Christians have ignored the warning of Jesus and succumbed to trying too hard in prayer, piling up words in empty repetition and naively imitating the latest techniques of 'powerful and prevailing prayer'. No Christian denomination or stream is entirely immune from the many excesses in which the externals of prayer come to dominate, whether in our vocabulary, our distinctive rhetorical style or our customary tone of voice.

As to vocabulary, many Christians who are perfectly capable of holding a normal conversation sink into strange archaisms as soon as they pray, lapsing into an antiquated use of thee, thou and thine. Some assume a strangely contrived eloquence, as if short words and sentences are unacceptable to God. Others indulge in peculiar circumlocutions: they pray for 'travelling mercies' rather than for a safe journey, for someone 'laid on a bed of sickness' rather than for someone who is ill. Still others lapse into constant repetition of a key word. There is the sincere prayer – 'We really do pray that we will really . . . .' There is the just prayer – 'We just pray that we will just . . . .' And then there is the sincere and just prayer – 'We really do just pray that we will really just . . . .' As to tone of voice, some become unctuously religious, oozing their requests in a strangely sonorous manner. Some become emphatically over-assertive, as if they were a sergeant major addressing a squad of unruly minor angels on a celestial parade ground. Some are unable to pray without shouting, even when praying for the gentle peace of Christ, as if there is a direct connection between volume and effectiveness; between the number of decibels and the degree of anointedness. Finally, still others indulge a trendy over-familiarity, demonstrating their 'street cred' by imitating a drug-dazed incoherence, stumbling out their enthusiasm for a God who is 'like, uh, well, so cool'.

Individuals can be excused a great deal of eccentricity. But when a whole church embraces a particular artificiality, when everyone conforms to the house style of 'proper praying', there is an undeniable problem. Because none of us wants to pray in the wrong way, we pick up the unwritten rules of public praying almost by osmosis. What we need is sufficient gentle humour to prick the idle pretensions of our meaningless conventions and techniques. Prayer is not about piling up words like the pagans. Prayer is about relationship. And that means there is a freedom to pray naturally, freed from anyone's artificial rules and regulations. Much of the style and effort of our praying has more to do with the foibles and follies of the pagans than with the direct simplicity of Jesus.

At its most innocent, copying the artificial ways in which others pray reveals no more than a naive enthusiasm to learn from others and do our best. At their worst, these techniques become a power game. Dickens recognised this in his satirical portrait of Mr Chadband, who employed fatuous repetition to endow himself with a spurious spirituality in the eyes of his acolytes. The irony of Dickens' concluding observation is deliciously acidic:

'My friends,' says Mr Chadband, 'Peace be on this house. On the master thereof, on the mistress thereof, on the young maidens, and on the young men! My friends, why do I wish for peace? What is peace? Is it war? No. Is it strife? No. Is it lovely, and gentle, and beautiful, and pleasant, and serene, and joyful? Oh yes! Therefore, my friends, I wish for peace, upon you and upon yours.' . . . The persecutors denied that there was any particular gift in Mr Chadband's piling verbose flights of stairs, one upon another, after this fashion. But this can only be received as a proof of their determination to persecute, since it must be within everyone's experience, that the Chadband style of oratory is widely received and much admired. (*Bleak House*, chapter 19)

Jesus' alternative approach is disarmingly simple and direct: 'Do not be like them, for your Father knows what you need before you ask him' (Mt 6:8). There is no suggestion that the Father guarantees to give us what we want. If every request was fulfilled immediately, many of us would never dare to pray again. The responsibility would be too great, the consequences of a foolish prayer too dangerous. What is promised is that the Father knows our every need. Our requests can therefore begin to flow from relationship, knowing that the Father loves us, despite our every failing, and that he understands our personal needs more precisely than we can ever understand ourselves.

In prayer we need to learn to relax, liberated from contrived vocabulary, strangulated voices or pursuing the latest in prayer techniques. Speaking in a way that comes naturally, we address the one who is the majestic Lord of the cosmos, and yet reveals himself to us in Christ as Abba, Father. Just as a young child can be relaxed and secure in the arms of their dad, we can discover security and intimacy in the love of God. He is no distant deity, busy with other responsibilities in the way that Elijah caricatured the god of the Baalites. And this Father in heaven, full of love, already knows our every need. Christian prayer has nothing to do with rousing the reluctant, nor informing the ignorant. Our prayers bring humble requests in a climate of love and security, trust and peace. It is time to enjoy being liberated from the strenuous and sterile futility of pagan styles of praying. Jesus encourages us to stop trying too hard when we pray.

The Believers' Prayer

The Lord's Prayer has long since been adopted within Western culture as a universal prayer. When I was very young I remember being given a book in which each double-page spread had one line of the Lord's Prayer accompanied by a suitable full colour illustration. Children were expected to read the book aloud as a bed-time prayer. Princess Diana's funeral in September 1997 demonstrated the extent to which it has remained the definitive prayer in the national psyche: many thousands of people in London parks joined in the prayer as the service was broadcast from Westminster Abbey.

The greatest threat to the prayer is probably the decline of the Authorised Version and the *Book of Common Prayer*. None of the modern versions has achieved universal acceptance, so the Lord's Prayer has generally fallen into disuse at large interdenominational gatherings, presumably for fear that the public declaration of the universal prayer of the church is likely to degenerate into a confusing cacophony of alternative phrases. More work needs to be done to establish fully a standardised form of the Lord's Prayer fit for the twenty-first century.

The language of the prayer is first person plural throughout

– *our* Father, *our* bread, *our* debts and so on. This indicates that the early Christians used this prayer together, although the content is equally applicable to the individual praying on their own. The prayer is therefore universal in the fullest sense, wholly appropriate as a public and corporate prayer, but equally valuable for private and personal use.

John Bunyan recognised that Jesus' words provide a rich and instructive framework for our own prayers, helping us to avoid an approach that becomes too limited, narrow or self-centred. However, Bunyan thoroughly overstated his case when he tried to argue that it was solely an outline and should never be used as an actual prayer. These magnificent words serve us in two complementary ways, both as a prayer in their own right and also as an outline for wholesome praying.

By immediately referring to the Father, the opening clause emphasises the approach that lies at the heart of Jesus' distinctive teaching about relationship with God. Through Jesus we can know God as Abba, Father, with a new intimacy and directness. The use of 'our' brings out the corporate consequences of personal faith. A new relationship with God as Father results in a new bond with fellow believers, who have become our brothers and sisters. The combination of 'Father' and 'heaven' embraces the creative tension between two key elements in Jesus' understanding of God. Immanence and intimacy in response to God's fatherhood combine with transcendence and awe in response to God's essential otherness, in holiness, majesty and might.

The early church would almost certainly not have approved of modern usage of the Lord's Prayer. Diana's funeral demonstrated an underlying assumption that this is a universal prayer, irrespective of personal faith. However, Jesus did not give this prayer to the wider Jewish community, but specifically to his disciples. The New Testament consistently argues that it is only by personal, saving faith in

Christ that we are brought into a new relationship with God as Father, adopted into the family of heaven. From the *Didache,* a first-century manual of Christian teaching, we discover that the first Christians reserved both participation in Communion and the use of the Lord's Prayer for those who had come to faith and been baptised. From its very first phrase it only really makes sense in the context of personal faith and living discipleship. The Lord's Prayer is therefore better described as the Believers' Prayer.

The rule of three which is found throughout Jesus' parables and teaching is also found within this noble prayer. After an opening phrase of address, there are two groups of three statements: three about God's impact on human destiny and then three about God's provision for our needs. The first trio of clauses prays for God's name, his kingdom and his will. *God's name is hallowed* – that is, revered and declared holy – by devoted worship and willing obedience. *The coming of God's kingdom* is inaugurated in the ministry of Jesus, advanced step by step through the dedication of his followers, and completed in the event of Jesus' return. This second request can be seen to embrace the broad implications of the kingdom in the teaching of Jesus, making our own lives available for the service and growth of the kingdom, while praying that God would hasten the final day. *God's will,* which we pray will be fulfilled in the third petition, is his eternal good purpose, revealed in the Scriptures and made manifest in the life of his Son. This is therefore a request for divine intervention, overcoming the tyranny of evil on the face of the earth, but also a prayer of submission, a willing surrender to the wise authority of our heavenly Father.

The first trio of petitions is followed by a phrase that should be understood to apply to all three and not just to the third – 'on earth as it is in heaven'. This explanatory clause helps us to understand the time frame of these first three requests. First, they are statements of praise for the eternally established condition of heaven: God's name is already and unreservedly hallowed, his will is fulfilled and his kingdom is gloriously complete. Second, they are statements about the final destiny of the human race: these three purposes will be brought to completion at the end of the age. Third, they are statements about present-day discipleship: the partial but developing expression of God's eternal purposes in the disciple's living faith and practical obedience. Jesus' prayer therefore encompasses the present and the future. Today's unspectacular process of steady growth in daily discipleship is the subject of this prayer at the same time as the once-for-all consummation that is yet to come.

In his second trio of petitions, Jesus shifts the focus to our personal needs and God's provision. A subsistence farmer tending his sparse crop and wondering whether the annual rains will fail is likely to relate to the request for daily bread with more urgency than a modern Westerner whose food is reliably available from the local supermarket. Nonetheless, the universal principle is established of our dependence upon God's provision. Bread was a staple form of carbohydrate for Galilean peasants – their equivalent of rice or potatoes. A prayer for bread is a request for sufficient food, for the essentials in life, not caviare and champagne. In the request for daily bread there is a deliberate echo of Israel's wilderness experience. They depended on God for a fresh provision of manna each day, and those who greedily gathered extra wasted their time, for overnight it became infested with maggots (Exod 16:20). The Believers' Prayer is not ashamed to recognise our daily need for food, for Jesus' spirituality embraces every aspect of life. The kingdom of heaven can never be locked up in a pigeon hole called 'Sunday mornings only'. The concept of self-reliance is entirely alien to the spirit of the prayer, for Jesus encourages us to acknowledge with humble submission our creaturely dependence upon God; explicitly for daily sustenance, implicitly in every aspect of life.

One further implication of this prayer for daily bread cannot be avoided. Once we have acknowledged dependence upon God for our own sufficiency, we are immediately implicated in the fulfilment of this prayer for others. Where we have more than enough food, our surplus should not be consumed to increase the problems of Western obesity, stored in grain silos or butter mountains, or even destroyed. It should be released to feed the hungry. Where our society has developed agricultural skills that can improve the harvest, these skills need to be transferred as cheaply and quickly as possible to the developing world so that their prayer for daily bread can be answered through more effective farming methods.

While the literal translation of 'daily bread' is obvious, it is not the only meaning here in Jesus' prayer. He presented himself as the 'Bread of life', and spoke of the need to feed upon him. 'Daily bread' therefore also speaks of daily spiritual sustenance, sometimes but not exclusively expressed through the breaking of bread in Communion. When quoting the Old Testament during his temptations, Jesus also affirmed that men and women do not live by bread alone, but by every word that comes from God (Mt 4:4). 'Daily bread' is therefore not a request that narrowly addresses bodily appetites, but it implicitly acknowledges our need for daily feeding upon Christ, by Word and Spirit.

The phrase 'daily bread' can also be translated 'bread for the coming day'. This helps us to recognise that the *present and future* dynamic of the first half of the prayer is sustained. 'Bread for the coming day' not only speaks of literal bread and spiritual sustenance for the very next day, but also looks forward to sustenance in days of persecution, and ultimately to participation in the great messianic banquet at the end of time.

The second of these three petitions concerning God's provision for our needs turns to forgiveness. The Aramaic word for debt was often used to mean 'sin', with the understanding that our offences against God's law create a debt of guilt that needs to be repaid. Matthew translates the Aramaic word literally, using the Greek word for 'debt', while Luke conveys the original meaning by using the word 'sins'. Jesus takes it for granted that his followers will have spiritual debts to clear, not just at the beginning of their discipleship, but every time they use this prayer. Confession and repentance are by no means restricted to our point of entry to the Christian faith, but remain an integral part of our continuing discipleship. For as long as we retain a sinful nature, the inner fight continues and so we go on praying for fresh forgiveness.

The availability of forgiveness is conditional. This principle is so important that Jesus provides an elaboration immediately after teaching this prayer. Within the prayer it may at first appear that a chronological order is implied: first we forgive others and only then will God grant forgiveness to us. This seems to turn God's forgiveness into a reward, conferred only upon those who have accomplished the task of first forgiving others. The real intention is subtly different. What Jesus is seeking to establish is not a chronology of forgiveness, but the fact that the two dimensions of forgiveness are directly and inextricably interconnected. As Manson observed, 'Nothing more surely shuts out a man from love than a censorious and unforgiving disposition. He who will not forgive closes his own heart against God's forgiveness.'

Faced with this uncompromising phrase in Jesus' prayer, it is not enough to acknowledge in principle the importance of forgiving others, nor to express the intention of getting around to forgiving them eventually. What Jesus requires of us is an unreserved declaration that the debts of others have been cleared completely. The aorist tense that Matthew employs is not restricted to a description of actions in the distant past, nor is it merely a sentimental expression of good intentions. It is a present statement of completed action that expresses full and final forgiveness for past sins. The book is closed. Their debt is now history. In the middle of his model prayer Jesus therefore includes an immediate requirement that is unequivocal. To pray the prayer authentically, we must relinquish all unforgiveness even as we pray. 'As we have forgiven them' carries the following meaning: 'I hereby declare that, as of this moment, I have entirely forgiven anyone who has sinned against me.' The person who recites the Lord's Prayer decorously, then scowls in disapproval at their rival in another pew, has wasted their breath. No forgiveness, no prayer.

Jesus' final phrase turns to temptation. The Greek word can equally mean 'being tempted to sin' or 'a time of trial'. 'Time of trial' in turn has three layers of meaning: extremely difficult personal circumstances; a time of persecution for the whole church; and the final time of testing before the end of the age (Mt 24:9). Once again the prayer encompasses the present and the future, the circumstances and prospects, both personal and corporate, of Jesus' disciples. There is no suggestion that God tempts us directly or takes pleasure in imposing trials upon his church. 'Lead us not into' means 'protect us from'. We can paraphrase the petition in this way: 'Preserve us from being overwhelmed by a tidal wave of temptation, difficult circumstances or persecution that is too great for us to resist.' The second part of this petition – 'deliver us from evil' – once again has present and future implications. In the present, we request that the hand of evil is restrained, which is another way of praying for protection from temptations and trials. As to the future, we confidently anticipate our absolute deliverance, when evil will be vanquished for all eternity.

The first trio of petitions captures the essence of God's impact upon humanity and our rightful response: willing devotion, eager availability and wholehearted surrender. The second trio of requests expresses a life-encompassing dependence upon God: seeking the Father's provision, forgiveness and protection. The entire prayer is unmistakably shot through with the presence of the future, for Jesus invites us to pray for the needs of today in the light of the coming of his kingdom. This is a prayer of revolution – not a decorous spirituality that leaves most of life untouched, but a prayer that engages us in nothing less than whole-life discipleship. The Believers' Prayer should have a spiritual safety warning attached. Once we really begin to pray in this way, our lives will never be the same again.

Prayer and forgiveness

Although forgiveness finds clear expression within the Believers' Prayer, this principle is so crucial to Jesus that he gives it special emphasis in the conclusion to this block of teaching about prayer. Two assumptions underlie the priority of forgiveness. First, we will continue to need the Father's forgiveness. Second, we will continue to need to forgive others. The apostle Paul brings the need for forgiveness close to home with his guidelines for positive relationships within the church: 'Bear with each other and forgive whatever grievances you may have against one another' (Col 3:13).

Similar implications are unmistakable. We all need to be forgiven and to forgive from time to time, and others may occasionally even find us unbearable! Many local churches would be much healthier and more pleasant communities if the discipline of forgiveness was rigorously practised. Forgiveness is not an optional extra – something to offer only in the case of minor offences, or something to get round to eventually. We need to keep short accounts and cultivate forgetfulness, for love does not keep a record of old wrongs (1 Cor 13:5). The time for forgiveness and forgetfulness is now.

Anyone who has been involved in providing pastoral care will have come to understand something of the dynamics of unforgiveness. First, unforgiveness is slavery to sin, not gospel freedom, for it refuses to know anything of grace and self-giving love.

Second, just as one rotten apple in a bowl of fruit needs to be removed before the entire bowlful is spoiled, unforgiveness turns bitter and spreads. We may begin by nursing a single grievance, but we then find it increasingly easy to take offence. As the unforgiveness breeds in our hearts, we compile a growing catalogue of grievances and offenders.

Third, unforgiveness makes us a present victim of past offence, for as long as we refuse to forgive, our negative attitude builds a bridge to the past, keeping alive the emotions of the original offence. As a result, the pain of the original experience walks across the bridge and continues to bring us hurt in the present. When we forgive, the emotional bridge is shattered and the hurt we have suffered is at last consigned to the past.

Fourth, unforgiveness can arise from others' actions or our own. Sometimes the person I have to choose to forgive is myself. This is particularly true for perfectionists, who have to learn to stop setting themselves impossible mountains to climb, and also for those who feel they have failed God and themselves in a particularly extreme manner. In such circumstances, Protestants have to recover the value of absolution, expressing in the name of Christ to the repentant the forgiveness which they find it so hard to believe and receive when confessing their sin in private.

Fifth, unforgiveness can arise from disappointed hopes, unfulfilled ambitions or even the frustrations of diminishing powers in old age. It is possible to project our negative emotions onto an individual or even an entire generation, blaming them for our feelings of being passed by or neglected.

Sixth, unforgiveness can arise on behalf of someone close to us. I remember vividly one woman who felt her husband had been badly treated by a church many years before. When he immediately decided to forgive, she was infuriated. Without telling her husband, she resolved in her heart that if he failed to stand up for himself, she would nurse a grievance on his behalf. This second-hand unforgiveness can become a terrible snare for husbands and wives, parents and children, brothers and sisters, good friends and even close colleagues. Choosing not to forgive on behalf of someone else may appear noble, but in reality it does no good for those we are seeking to defend, and ultimately it becomes self-destructive.

Seventh, forgiveness begins with the will and not with the feelings. We forgive when and because we choose to forgive. Jesus does not invite us to neglect forgiveness until we feel like it. The example of Christ should emblazon upon our heart and mind the need to make the first move, always offering forgiveness and seeking reconciliation. Paul summed up succinctly the inspiring example of the cross of Christ: 'Forgive as the Lord forgave you' (Col 3:13).

For some, Jesus' call to forgiveness may seem impossible, almost cruel. The victims of deep, grievous wounding and even criminal hurts need to receive compassionate and confidential support, not glib, instant and superficial solutions. Jesus does not suggest that forgiveness will always be easy, but he does insist that it is ultimately necessary. Forgiveness is sometimes a journey that must be walked painfully, one step at a time. The task of those providing pastoral support is neither to condemn nor to rush the victim, but to provide companionship and assistance as the journey into forgiveness is advanced.

The interconnectedness of our relationships is explicit and emphatic in Jesus' teaching. If we do not forgive men and women, we cannot know the forgiveness of the Father. This brings home the tragic absurdity of those who are devoted in prayer and yet also continue to nurse a grievance. Jesus is completely uncompromising: our relationship with God cannot be right for as long as we store up unforgiveness. Paul makes a similar point when he explains that having negative attitudes towards other Christians grieves the Spirit (Eph 4:30). It is quite impossible to cultivate an intimate and positive prayer life while we walk in unforgiveness. If we become sour and crabby, negative and critical towards others, it will inevitably paralyse our relationship with God. Unforgiveness poisons prayer.

Unforgiveness is an emotional quagmire in which we can become trapped for years. More than that, Jesus warns us emphatically that the spiritual consequences are dire, destroying the possibility of true intimacy with the Father, with the result that we can no longer enjoy the gift of divine forgiveness and restoration. The urgent and persuasive invitation of Jesus' teaching beckons us to a better way of life. We need to ensure that our eyes dwell less upon the offence of others than upon our own quest for purity of heart and closeness to the Father. Jesus calls us to a life distinguished by the willingness and speed with which we extend the gift of forgiveness to others. Only then can we begin to explore Jesus' provision of a new spirituality: intimacy with the Father and true freedom in prayer.

II

Freedom from Materialism and Anxiety
Matthew 6:19–34

When a group of strangers come together for a day con-
ference it can be good to start the day with an ice-breaker.
One good way to ease people into discussion is to invite
them to introduce themselves through an exercise such as
this: 'If you were able to keep only one of your possessions,
what would it be?' Our prized possession can reveal a lot
about us. As we describe it, and explain why it is so special to
us, we give others a much fuller impression of our personality than through a more formal introduction.

Enjoying our possessions and expressing our own identity
through them seems to be instinctive, an intrinsic part of
being human. Problems begin to arise when we lose a
healthy perspective on life and develop a disproportionate,
even obsessive, concern with material acquisitions. Our
emotional and spiritual well-being is at risk as soon as our
possessions become our ultimate concern. One American
businessman summed up his devotion to the god of consumerism: 'The three priorities in my life are God, family
and work, and in my office the order is reversed.'

Jesus exposed the drivenness of a life built around a
constant effort to win religious approval, and invited his
followers to discover a new freedom from human religion

(Mt 6:1–18). Now he similarly exposes the drivenness of constant striving for more material things and invites his followers to discover a new freedom from materialism and anxiety (6:19–34). Just as the six messianic intensifications (Mt 5:21–48) follow from the call for a higher righteousness (Mt 5:20), the prospect of liberation from materialism and anxiety follows from the Lord's or, more accurately, the Believers' Prayer. An experience of liberation from materialism and anxiety can be described as the Believers' Prayer in action, for a new lifestyle will emerge when we really believe what Jesus taught us to pray.

Nothing could be more pertinent for our society, in which shopping malls have become great temples of conspicuous consumption. Descartes concluded that the gift of reason is central to what it means to be human – to think is to be. Sartre's existentialism placed a new emphasis on self-assertion through action – to do is to be. As the twentieth century comes to an end, the great cities of the Western world demonstrate a new centre to our sense of identity – to shop is to be, *tesco ergo sum*.

Materialism makes the world go round. It is the blood in the veins of the acquisitive society. Materialism is not just about having possessions. It is a way of life and a complete set of values. Our culture is built upon the latest, the most modern, the disposable. A few years ago everyone seemed to be installing new bathrooms. Replacement kitchens were not far behind. And then the modernised bathroom needed replacing, because the deep avocado colour that was once the height of fashion had become irredeemably out of date. We are a society built upon instant credit and instant gratification. We buy in haste and repent six weeks later when the credit card bill arrives.

As a result of our materialistic drivenness, life is ever more busy and the treadmill never stops. All available energy is channelled into getting on and getting more. But someone needs to blow the whistle on our ever more frenetic quest for material gain. No one ever made this statement as their death-bed regret: 'I wish I'd spent more time in the office.'

Treasure on earth

Although the two dominant themes inevitably overlap, this part of the Sermon on the Mount falls naturally into two sections: materialism (6:19–24) and then anxiety (6:25–34). Liberation from materialism can be seen as a commentary upon the second clause of the Believers' Prayer: 'Your kingdom come.' Liberation from anxiety is a commentary or elaboration upon the fourth clause: 'Give us this day our daily bread.' The section on materialism is particularly robust, for Jesus will allow no compromise with the love of money.

Within his polemic against materialism, Jesus sets up three stark contrasts: treasure in heaven or treasure on earth; good eyes that provide inner light or bad eyes that provide inner darkness; two incompatible masters, God and Mammon. First Jesus warns against the futility of a life devoted to storing up treasure on earth, stockpiling more and more in pursuit of happiness and fulfilment. Do I have a big enough house? Is my mortgage rate low enough, my savings rate high enough? The catch word is *enough*. Where money rules, there is never enough. All our energy can be devoted to securing one special new possession. Some years ago a new model Ford Escort was released to great fanfares of publicity. There was a Ford dealer near our house, so we passed their proud display of gleaming Escorts every time we travelled home from the supermarket. Eventually we bought one, and were the proudest of owners. Within a few months they brought out new styling. Then we began to look at larger models. Satisfaction is always around the corner that never comes.

Money always promises more than it delivers, offering hope of fulfilment tomorrow, but there is always something more to buy. 'Once we're settled in, we'll begin to give more money to charity.' But then the car goes wrong, or you need new curtains. Seneca summed up the trauma of a society driven by consumerism when he observed: 'The most grievous kind of destitution is to want money in the midst of wealth.' Money is like salt water. The more we drink, the thirstier we become.

Richard Burton gave a memorable interview to the BBC not long before he died. One of the greatest actors of his generation, he had been reduced to making bad films for big money. He revealed that there were years in which he earned several million dollars and promptly spent the lot. Towards the end of the interview he made an unforgettable remark about the isolation he had been left with following such extravagance: 'I don't trust people. I can count on the fingers of one hand the people I trust.' Money promised happiness and fulfilment. Its lasting legacy was loneliness, cynicism and the need for more money. Thomas Carlyle, the great Victorian social commentator, came to a gloomy conclusion: 'For every hundred men who can stand adversity, there is only one who can stand prosperity.'

The governing principle of materialism is that we must be dissatisfied today in order to spend even more tomorrow. We are a society driven and restless in the constant pursuit of more. Magpies, those relentless scavengers of the natural world, have nothing on dedicated materialists. The free newspapers that come tumbling through our doors each week demonstrate that there is always someone somewhere ready to sell us something we haven't yet bought. Until we saw the latest adverts, we didn't even realise that our life was incomplete without the new improved models of our household and office equipment. I saw a gardening programme recently that gave some surprising advice: 'Don't forget to stop and enjoy your garden.' It seems that we are so busy getting more, we're forgetting to enjoy what we've already got.

Advertising fuels the fires of materialism, and we cannot escape its siren voice, from TV and radio, magazines, billboards and sports sponsorship. It tells us not merely what's new, but implies that without the latest we cannot be really happy. We won't be loved. We're so out of touch we're positively Jurassic. And, worst of all, without the latest we are deliberately neglecting our children, depriving them of those things that will guarantee them success later in life.

Jesus identifies the immediate and inevitable threats to treasure on earth – moths, rust and thieves – but he declines to spell out the inescapable reality that whatever treasure escapes these earthly assailants will have to be surrendered to death. Instead Jesus emphasises the alternative option: treasure in heaven that is permanent and secure. From Jesus' perspective, there is simply no comparison between the two kinds of treasure. A life devoted to treasure on earth is simply unreasonable.

This first contrast is established and stark, but Jesus adds a further saying about treasure that stands on its own as a severe and disturbing warning: 'For where your treasure is, there your heart will be also' (Mt 6:21). Jesus' words are simple but searching. There can be only one ultimate concern in our lives, one centre of gravity. If I profess to follow Jesus, but my energy is devoted to the pursuit of treasure on earth, I am a disciple in name only, for my heart is still set on material prosperity. The choice Jesus sets before his disciples deliberately has no grey areas. There is only one location for storing treasure, only one destiny on which our heart can be set.

A similar starkness is found in the following mini-parable about good and bad eyes. The contrast is rather more tortuous than Jesus' usual style, but the essential meaning is clear. Our perspective on life is fundamentally determined by the nature of our ultimate concern. Driven materialists have a constrictive, distorted and ultimately destructive way of looking at life. What Jesus offers in the Sermon on the Mount is a new way of seeing. The kingdom of heaven provides Jesus' disciples with a different perspective on the perennial and compulsive human quest for treasure on earth.

Serving Mammon

Jesus' third contrast begins with a mini-parable that offers as self-evident the conclusion that no one can serve two masters. This is a skilful rhetorical device: the general principle receives willing endorsement from Jesus' audience, and then he springs the trap. His real point is not to pass comment on the employment situation, but to demand absolute and single-minded loyalty to the kingdom of heaven. The initial premise of the problem of holding down two jobs begins to be left behind in the extremity of the contrast that Jesus draws: *hating* one and *loving* the other. The term Mammon can be found in rabbinic writings with the neutral meaning 'material possessions'. Jesus sharpens the term to mean 'a driven love of material possessions'; that is, materialism. Mammon should not be thought of as a named demonic power. Jesus is simply personifying the love of material possessions. In search of a modern equivalent, the following are possibilities: you cannot serve both God and Manhattan; you cannot serve both God and the Dow Jones Index; you cannot serve both God and the Square Mile. Jesus' contrast allows no shades of grey. He demands total allegiance and insists that materialism must be recognised as an implacable enemy of the kingdom of heaven.

Four interconnected and profoundly life-diminishing consequences arise whenever materialism becomes our master. First, *materialism sets restricted horizons for our lives*, suggesting that possessions matter far more than anything else. Materialism produces a desperately cramped and dehumanised view of people and of what really matters in life. Value and fulfilment come to be measured solely in monetary terms. A Texan multi-millionaire summed up the approach to life in which money had become everything: 'If it don't make money, it ain't pretty.' Love of money destroys our true dignity. It reduces us from rounded people to narrowly focused consumers. A friend of ours was interviewed for a job and was asked: 'What do you want from life in ten years' time?' The only answer they were interested in was to do with the size of salary.

Money, it has been said, is made round to slip through our fingers. When money speaks, truth is silent. It can buy everything except love, and pay the fare to every place except heaven. Naturally most of us hate too much money – especially whenever someone else is spending it. The New Testament warns that the love of money is a root of all evil (1 Tim 6:10). Most of us have had some kind of unpleasant encounter with that love. Christians often have cause to disagree with the assertions of Bertrand Russell, but there is much truth in his stark warning about materialism: 'It is preoccupation with possessions more than anything else that prevents men from living freely and nobly.'

Second, *materialism excludes the poor*. The population of the Two-Thirds World controls less and less of the world's total wealth. We buy their resources cheaply. We encourage them to buy prestigious military equipment rather than the technology that would promote sustained development. We destroy or hoard our surplus crops to keep prices high. Research into genetically manipulated plants may result in even higher yields in developed countries, so the South may not even be able to sell us as many cash crops.

The Brandt Report recognised that the world's poor are getting poorer. Up to one third of all children die from malnutrition-related diseases by the age of five. The Brandt Commission proposed new approaches to world development. The emphasis was not on charity and handouts, but on enlightened self-interest. Real development in the developing countries of the South would enable the industrialised North to find new markets. But the leaders of the world's most powerful economies dumped the proposals. It is to be hoped that the present Jubilee 2000 campaign for reducing international debts will not suffer the same fate.

One third of the world consumes two-thirds of the world's resources. There is more than enough food in the world, but most of it is eaten in countries where obesity is a growing problem and diet books are regular bestsellers. The macro-economic problems are immensely complex, but materialism is the distorted perspective that causes us conveniently to ignore the plight of the poor.

Third, *materialism ignores ecology*. Planet earth is God's gift and our responsibility. We are destroying the world's non-renewable resources in order to indulge a frivolous lifestyle. Rain forests, mineral deposits and wildlife are all in devastating decline. Springtime across Europe is growing quieter with every passing year, for intensive farming has decimated the population of songbirds as we poison their environment through the indiscriminate use of pesticides, and destroy their habitat by tearing down ancient hedgerows and woods. The glorious resources of the natural order were created by God for the benefit and pleasure of all people. Materialism treats them like an unlimited overdraft, but credit is running out fast. One of the worst offenders is the United States, with President Clinton consistently failing to agree to the anti-pollution targets proposed by the more enlightened nations. In their obdurate refusal to legislate a rapid reduction in carbon monoxide emissions, American capitalism and Chinese Marxism have entered a polluters' pact and set their faces against the future viability of planet earth.

Above all, *materialism marginalises God*. Love of money pushes God to the religious margins of life, an optional hobby for Sunday mornings so long as we can find a more convenient time to get to Sainsbury's. When Jesus met one rich young man, he saw at once that he was enmeshed in the love of money (Mt 19:16–24). His love of money was so strong that Jesus advised him to sell all he had and give everything to the poor. That advice was not given to everyone, but Jesus was quite prepared to give it when needed. It is salutary for Westerners in this generation to reflect on this infamous young man. He had no access to many of the possessions that most of us take for granted as the bare necessities of life. But the possessions and wealth he did enjoy held him like a vice so that he was entirely unable to break free and become a disciple of Jesus. Materialism promises to make us special, but the price it can exact is immense: first our freedom, and ultimately even our soul.

Jesus' home truths about making material things our ultimate concern do not mean that TVs or videos, freezers or microwaves need to be outlawed by the dedicated disciple. But we need to recognise that consumerism can make hidden demands upon us that have severe consequences. A materialistic lifestyle is dangerous. If we lose sight of the eternal, and devote our lives to the narrow pursuit of treasure on earth, our devotion of heart may eventually prove terminal to our spiritual health.

Escape from anxiety

Jesus now turns to the Achilles' heel of materialism. When material possessions become our gods, life becomes consumed with anxiety. Three times in Matthew 6 Jesus repeats his wise counsel: 'Therefore I tell you, do not worry' (v.25);

'So do not worry' (v.31); 'Therefore do not worry' (v.34). The frequency of this repetition underlines Jesus' conviction that worry about material things is parasitic. It serves no real purpose, but sucks energy from our lives.

The classic focal points of worry that Jesus identifies are all too familiar today. They represent the three great themes of advertising and many monthly magazines: What shall we eat? What shall we drink? What shall we wear? (Mt 6:25, 31). Most of us are indeed inclined to worry about our food and clothes. If we don't worry about having sufficient food and clothes, we worry about additives and calories or fashionable styles and colours. The pursuit of material possessions always leads to worry.

The trio of anxieties identified by Jesus indicates a lifestyle obsessed with externals, with creating an image or keeping up appearances. According to most analysts, the postmodern condition of Western culture is putting increasing energy into precisely these concerns. We are driven by a pleasure principle which pursues ever greater highs and ever more exotic food and holidays. We are also driven by the suggestion that we can reconstruct the self, renewing our self-worth, by creating a new image. It is no longer just Madonna who reinvents herself every few years. A whole generation of young adults are being invited to make the same journey. A recent advert for soap powder summed up this externalisation of self: when your clothes look good, you feel good. Our culture has become so preoccupied with externals that we have allowed a vacuum to emerge within. The cultivation of the inner self, the exploration of our spirituality, these more profound and enduring elements of the human condition have been largely ignored in the West through several decades of dedication to materialistic superficiality.

Jesus not only urges his disciples to renounce the way of anxiety, he castigates its folly. First, he argues that consumer-driven anxiety is profoundly trivial: 'Is not life more important?' (6:25). The very fact of such anxiety demonstrates a loss of perspective, a disproportionate energy being directed into concerns that are ultimately secondary. Jesus does not suggest that dowdiness is next to godliness. He does not imply that material possessions are intrinsically sinful. He does not impose upon every disciple the response of Francis of Assisi, who stripped naked in the public square and renounced his inheritance. But Jesus does urge us to retain a due sense of proportion: our life's orbit should be centred around the priorities of the kingdom of heaven, the prospect of eternal life and the practice of the love commands. We are relational beings made in the image of God, not ravenous consumers living only for food, drink and fashion.

Jesus' second critique of worry pinpoints its impotence. No one ever added an hour to life through worrying (6:27). We now know, of course, that quite the reverse is true. Anxiety and stress can lead to increased blood pressure and heart problems, to raised levels of stomach acid and risks of ulceration, to sleep disorders and sexual dysfunction. We can also distinguish two types of worry – on the one hand worry about a specific problem, on the other a free-floating anxiety state. Free-floating anxiety identifies a focus for its churning emotions, but as soon as that particular issue is resolved another problem is latched onto in its place. The levels of anxiety remain more or less constant, but the notional reason or justification for the feelings keeps changing. The experience is like walking through marshland: free one foot from the sucking mud and with your next step you promptly begin to sink again. Those who suffer from this condition will easily identify their symptoms. The key is not condemnation but wise counsel, for they desperately need to escape from the marshes of free-floating anxiety.

Jesus' third critique of materialistic anxiety exposes its universality: 'The pagans run after all these things' (6:32).

Once again Jesus reminds his disciples that he is calling them to whole-life discipleship that requires a new way of seeing, a renewed set of priorities. He is deliberately using shock tactics: if we share the burning anxieties of a materialistic society, we are living as pagans, whatever our profession of faith. Jesus is not offering a discipleship that can be bolted onto our existing ambitions without changing them, as if we could become dedicated Christians and devout materialists simultaneously. He offers no halfway house, but calls us to total allegiance, to a radically different set of values that overthrows the pagan obsession with material things. To follow Jesus means to turn our backs on the superficial and selfish concerns of secular materialism. Any mutation of Christianity that encourages its followers to make a life priority of pursuing treasure on earth is a wicked and foolish contradiction of the Sermon on the Mount. Jesus repudiates unreservedly such pagan preoccupations and invites us instead to enter into his own glorious freedom from materialism and anxiety.

Resources for living

Alongside his penetrating critique of the anxiety that arises when materialism becomes our ultimate concern, Jesus provides a way of escape, a fourfold strategy that will release us from the treadmill of consumerism. First, *we can consider ourselves the crown of a creation that is cared for*. Just as God's response to Job turns the eyes of the sufferer from his own pain to the beauteous order of creation, Jesus encourages us to lift our eyes from materialistic obsessions to the birds of the air (6:26) and the lilies of the field (6:28–30). We have no way of knowing the time of year when Jesus preached his Great Sermon, but in spring the hills of Galilee are carpeted with a glorious abundance of absolutely stunning wild flowers. Even as he spoke his disciples may have glanced at their feet, seen the flame red and golden yellow blooms and readily agreed with Jesus' suggestion that not even Solomon's couturiers were any match for the Creator's artistry. Not only is creation cared for, but the care of God is extravagant. A flower that lasts a single day is not treated dismissively, but has beauty lavished upon it. A sense of God's abundant care arising from the contemplation of nature is infinitely more rewarding than a sense of anxiety arising from the contemplation of magazines devoted to fashion and food. To find our place in creation is to discover a source of tranquillity.

Second, *we need to be vigilant in evicting worry.* Jesus' threefold repetition concerning worry is more than a diagnosis of the connection between materialism and anxiety; it is also an unambiguous instruction. Here is no place for non-directive listening; for a neutral and non-judgemental response to someone else's preferred path through life. According to Jesus, materialistic anxiety is a destructive, invasive and ultimately dehumanising force, and so he emphatically commands its eviction without compromise or delay.

Third, *we need to consider ourselves no longer governed by life's normal priorities.* In absolute contrast with the obsessive scurrying of the pagans after materialistic gain, Jesus calls us to detachment. With a kingdom perspective, we are simply not prepared to allow life to be swallowed up by such matters. Food, drink and fashion will be kept in their place and we will not allow them to become our ultimate concern. At the same time, Jesus emphasises our new sense of security: 'Your heavenly Father knows that you need them.' A quiet trust in God's provision can replace a relentless pursuit of the latest and the best.

Fourth, *we need to discover the eternal focal point for life's energies.* What comes first, Jesus declares, is the Father's kingdom and righteousness (6:33). God's 'kingdom' means his rule, and that calls us to submission. God's 'righteousness' means his ways of purity and justice, and that calls us to practical obedience, both personally and in the values that we press upon our society. (For the societal impact of God's righteousness in terms of justice for the poor, see the earlier exploration of the fourth beatitude.) If two teams were to set off on a transatlantic yacht race and one had a faulty compass, the teams' prospects and journeys would be entirely different. Similarly Jesus offers to chart a completely new course through life for his followers. His priorities are neither sensible nor realistic from the point of view of a society built around selfishness and consumerism. God's kingdom and righteousness are the passions of a people marching to a different drummer. We turn a deaf ear to the siren voices of materialism, and choose instead the less-trodden path of radical non-conformity. Genuine discipleship will always appear extreme, because according to the wisdom of this world detachment from materialism can only be unpleasant and demeaning, while self-giving love seems too risky and costly.

A guarantee is attached to this new set of priorities: 'And all these things will be given to you as well' (6:33). This is no guarantee of materialistic abundance, but although none of the first Christian leaders lived a life of wealth and luxury, not one of them complained that the risen Christ had somehow let them down. Jesus' promise is that our essential needs will be met, without having to waste energy in worrying. Our instinctive, materialistic aspirations are another matter entirely. The whole force of Matthew 6 is that Jesus calls us to an absolute allegiance, a completely new set of priorities, an unqualified repudiation of the ways of Mammon, and a complete reconstruction of our dreams. We need to stop nurturing in ourselves and our children the same appetites as the pagans, and learn to cultivate a new hunger: God's rule and righteousness on the face of the earth.

Choosing freedom

Usually without even noticing, Western churches have often become ensnared in the web of materialism. More than 2.5 billion people in the world have never heard the gospel. Up to 1 billion are starving or malnourished. The so-called 'Christian countries' of Western Europe are full of people who don't know about the need for personal, saving faith in Jesus Christ. Materialism saps our time and energy. Mammon wants to leave little or no place in our lives for proclaiming the good news of Jesus Christ and living in the way of self-giving love as his disciples. Much of the Christian religion that is practised in the Western world is privately engaging but publicly irrelevant, locked away in a pietistic box that is only opened on Sundays.

We desperately need to learn how to match up our values against the teaching of Jesus. The remarkable testimony of the first Christians was a liberation from selfish materialism into a new sense of community. Individualistic consumerism simply cannot cope with Luke's astonishingly radical description of the early church: 'No-one claimed that any of his possessions was his own' (Acts 4:32). Materialism wriggles hastily away from Luke's admiring summary of the wonderful example they set: 'There were no needy persons among them' (Acts 4:34).

If we are to rediscover in practice Jesus' way of discipleship, the instinctive and engrained materialism of our culture needs to be nailed and nailed again to the cross of Christ. Jesus declared that he had come to set prisoners free. His call to discipleship continues to hold out the hope of a decisive liberation in this generation from the tyranny of consumerism. The Western church faces an urgent need for comprehensive and rigorous deliverance from the twin cries of the materialistic lifestyle: 'I want more!' and 'What's in it for me?'

Matthew 6 is Jesus' charter for freedom. He invites his followers to enter into a new liberation from three kinds of dehumanising bondage – the shallow conformity of human religion, the drivenness of materialism and the paralysis of constant anxiety. We can readily sum up Jesus' way of freedom: don't just pray the Believers' Prayer, live it!

PART FOUR

The Way of Right Relationships
Matthew 7

12

Right Relationships

Matthew 7

Right with others (Mt 7:1–6, 12)

I have never seen someone with a plank in their eye, but I have seen a tree performing the same function. When I was a young teenager we moved house, and my dad requested help in the new garden. We were planting a fruit tree, and the idea was that I should hold the upper branches steady while Dad added just enough soil to the hole into which we were going to set the roots. On his word of command, I was meant to lower the tree into the hole. For some strange reason, however, rather than simply move the tree downwards I decided to lift it a little first. And this was how, rather than planting the roots in the soil, I planted a branch in my father's eye. Fortunately he was not badly injured, but this brought to a sudden end my training in horticulture.

The stabbing pain of a splinter in the eye is absolutely agonising. Once the offending item has been removed, it can be very embarrassing to discover on the end of your finger no more than a tiny speck. The agony surely indicated something much larger! A first-century Jewish carpenter's workshop would no doubt be condemned as a disaster area by a modern health and safety inspector. To their eyes it would look like an accident waiting to happen. Presumably Jesus must have known personally the agony of a splinter or sawdust in the eye and the need to have someone else help remove the offending speck. Jesus' unforgettable mini-parable is taken directly from his former workplace, although neither Jesus, nor Joseph, nor any of Jesus' half-brothers would ever have seen someone with a whole plank in their eye. With this wonderfully vivid-yet-bizarre picture of a person suffering from what we might call 'optical enplankment', Jesus illustrates the opening principle of this final section: 'Do not judge.'

The final chapter of the Great Sermon is structurally connected to the rest of Jesus' message in several complementary ways. It continues to develop the call for a new righteousness that exceeds that of the Pharisees (Mt 5:20). It also picks up on Jesus' previous teaching about forgiveness: if liberation from materialism connects with the second clause of the Lord's Prayer about the coming kingdom (Mt 6:19–24 with 6:10), and liberation from resultant anxiety connects with the fourth about daily bread (Mt 6:25–34 with 6:11), this section on right relationships with one another naturally connects with the fifth clause, concerning forgiveness (Mt 7:1–6 with 6:12, 14–15). A third level of structural integration occurs within the last chapter itself, which is devoted to the theme of right relations. The first two sections present Jesus' distinctive intensification of the implications of the two love commands – loving God and loving one another. Jesus tackles these two themes in reverse order – right relations with one another (7:1–6) and then right relations with the Father (7:7–11). The interconnectedness of these two themes is emphasised by the way Jesus saves his Golden Rule about human relationships until after he has explored our relationship with the Father (7:12).

At this point in the Great Sermon Jesus' ethics of the kingdom of heaven have been taught in full and he has explored the two great dimensions of our relationships:

towards God and towards one another. What follows, however, completes the theme of how best to relate to others by
turning to right relationship with Jesus (7:13–27). Within
this third great and critical aspect of right relations comes an
additional subsection on right relations with false prophets
(7:15–23), although this section is itself focused upon these
people's wrong relationship with Jesus.

Jesus' picture of the man with a plank is so exaggerated as
to be a deliberate caricature. Here is a man deeply concerned about his brother's speck while unaware of his own
encumbrance. He not only remains completely oblivious to
the great beam, he even offers to help remove his brother's
speck. The notion is preposterous, so Jesus uses a harsh
rebuke: 'You hypocrite!' There should be a proper sense
of proportion, and dealing with the plank must take priority.
The conclusion to the parable is ambiguous. It could be
sarcastic and mean that once you remove the plank you
will see straight and be able to recognise there is no speck
at all in your brother's eye, but the meaning is probably less
tortuous: it is good to want to help your brother, but you
can only be of help if you sort yourself out first. Jesus'
calculated humour is designed to prick the bubble of our
pomposity and self-importance. If we are ever tempted to
take ourselves too seriously or to consider ourselves above
the common herd as we point out the problems of others
and offer help, this parable stands as a pointed warning:
beware the plank in your own eye!

The kind of judgement Jesus is rejecting, both in the
opening words of the chapter and in this sharply pointed
parable, is made clear by the context. He cannot possibly be
excluding every kind of judgement, since the mini-parable
demands that we judge ourselves in order to identify and
remove the plank in our own eye. Once we have completed
our own major surgery, we are in a position to provide
minor first aid for our brother or sister, which also requires

an act of judgement. The warning to avoid wasting sacred things and pearls on dogs and pigs (7:6) also requires discernment: to the Jews, dogs and pigs were considered unclean animals. In the *Didache*, a first-century manual of Christian instruction, this was interpreted to mean restricting the communion meal to believers and excluding any believers who were unrepentant sinners. But Jesus' warning about the need to exercise wise discrimination has much wider implications, making it applicable in any setting where people might despise or mock Christian worship, doctrine and practice.

Looking beyond the immediate context, when Jesus taught about church discipline he once again recognised a valid, indeed essential, dimension of discerning judgement (Mt 18:15–17). Similarly Paul gave clear instructions concerning the implementation of church discipline (1 Cor 5) and was quite prepared to warn Timothy against the destructive influence of a certain Alexander (2 Tim 4:14–15). Neither the immediate context nor the broader sweep of the New Testament allows us to interpret Jesus' words as a rigorous exclusion of every possible type of judgement. He says nothing that repudiates the necessary virtue of wise and gracious discernment which is sooner or later unavoidable for every parent and leader. What he is really excluding is finger-pointing, gossip, spitefulness, party spirit, cynicism, sharpness and negativity; that is, the wretched and destructive vice of judgementalism.

It is a terrible blight upon the church that a clique of judgementalists who have just shared in Communion with brothers and sisters will then lay into them over coffee or Sunday lunch. Like ravenous piranhas they savagely bite and tear at their prey, discussing what is wrong with the minister, the musicians, the elders or PCC. This is not wise discernment of the kind Jesus commended; it is Christian cannibalism. If Jesus' words were taken seriously, no one would dare to indulge this vicious, verbal blood sport ever again. Jesus spells out the principle of reciprocity: the way we judge others will be the way we are judged; the measure we use will be the measure used against us (7:2). Such teaching should stop the mouths of judgementalists and gossips. Faced with such a daunting prospect, how dare we be so sweeping and cavalier in our judgement of others? The more we know that we need God to deal with us with mercy, patience and grace, the more these qualities should inform the way we respond to the deficiencies of others.

Jesus explores at some length the negative traits that need to be eradicated if we are to establish right relations with one another. He then holds back his Golden Rule until after exploring right relations with the Father. Jesus is clearly wanting to convey several important implications. The two dimensions of our right relationships – vertical and horizontal, with God and with one another – are not two isolated compartments. In fact they interact with one another. Not getting on well with a close friend is likely to have a prejudicial impact upon our relationship with God. The two dimensions need to be developed in parallel. It is an insufficient fulfilment of the Great Sermon to be close to God but intolerant of other people, or to be loving towards men and women but indifferent to God. Above all, the way we relate to others needs to be informed by the way in which God relates to us. By reserving the Golden Rule that sums up our brother–sister relationships until after exploring God's fatherliness towards us, Jesus provides his disciples with the framework of God's glorious generosity as a context and resource to inspire deepening relationships with one another.

And so we turn to Jesus' Golden Rule – the climax and summation of his ethical teaching; the one-sentence encapsulation of his messianic intensification of the Law: 'So in everything, do to others what you would have them do to you, for this sums up the Law and the Prophets' (7:12). Other great moral teachers, both Jewish and Gentile, had recognised the value of the negative formulation – don't do to others what you don't want them to do to you. Among the rabbis, Hillel offered this approach. Among the Greeks, the same practical wisdom came from the pen of Isocrates of Athens. Jesus' insight is so much more profound and demanding. He calls his followers not merely to avoid the negative, but to go the extra mile of self-giving love, and seek to contribute positively to the well-being of others.

Fine-tuned consideration of the needs of others is critical if we want to be successful in applying Jesus' rule. I heard about one family, where enjoying a box of chocolates always followed the same pattern: the mother opened the box and removed all the hard centres before handing around the remaining sweets. She then consumed every hard-centred chocolate herself. With the arrival of early teenage years, one daughter could stand this unequal distribution no longer and demanded to know why Mum always hogged the hard centres. The reply was unexpected: 'Because, dear, I don't like them, so I have always helped the rest of you enjoy the chocolates to the full by eating all the horrible ones.' Unfortunately her generosity backfired completely. The children actually preferred hard centres, so from their perspective their mum had consistently seemed to be greedy rather than self-sacrificing.

Jesus does not give us encouragement to impose upon others the exact manner in which we like to be treated. Otherwise brash extroverts would have a licence to appal and embarrass every reserved introvert whoever has the misfortune to cross their path. What Jesus calls us to is more subtle and demanding: to relate to others with the kind of precise personal touch with which we would like them to treat us. We should endeavour to customise our response to every individual we meet so that our manner is thoroughly fitting to their personality and needs, as individually tailored as possible.

Jesus describes his Golden Rule as a summary of the Law and the Prophets. Hillel had done the same for his negative rule: 'This is the whole law; all else is commentary.' This indicates that Jesus is not claiming absolute originality of thought for his interpretation of the Old Testament so much as definitive clarity. The personally tailored kindness of self-giving love according to the Golden Rule gets to the kernel of the intentions of the Old Testament. This completes the line of argument in the Sermon that began with Jesus' statement that he had come to fulfil the Law and the Prophets (Mt 5:17). Here the fulfilment is in terms of an interpretation that is comprehensively put into practice in Jesus' own life and to which he now calls his followers. Just as the Ten Commandments are the most succinct and complete law code ever written, providing a remarkably coherent and comprehensive moral foundation for any society, Jesus' Golden Rule is an unsurpassable one-sentence summary of biblical morality; his higher righteousness in a single sentence. He has provided a principle worthy of being applied in every situation – an ideal that will never cease to stretch its adherents to new efforts of self-sacrifice and servanthood. The more seriously we take the Golden Rule, the more our life will become a daily adventure of faith. Where love is our priority, there is always more to give.

Nothing could be more remote from the approach of the Pharisees. They concentrated on all the things you should not do as an individual, but Jesus emphasises the positive impact of God's demands upon our relationships. Positive holiness entails more than avoiding sin. Jesus calls us to embrace a new and higher righteousness of purity of heart and self-giving love. The Golden Rule should sum up the lifestyle of every local church. We are called to be the community of the Beatitudes, the community of the higher righteousness, the community of liberation and the community of brotherly and sisterly love.

Right with the Father (Mt 7:7–11)

The twin themes of relating to one another and relating to the Father are interwoven throughout Jesus' teaching. Once again, for the last time in the Great Sermon, Jesus returns to the theme of relating to the Father. First he provides a resounding affirmation of the effectiveness of prayer, echoing once more the petitionary aspect of the Lord's Prayer. Some have tried to suggest a developing narrative in this sequence, as if a new arrival in town, clutching an address in his hand, *asks* instructions of how to get to his desired destination. He then *seeks* the location, and when he finds it he finally *knocks* on the door for entry. We can recognise an undeniable logic to such a sequence, which serves to reinforce further the promise that prayer works. It helps make Jesus' repetition intuitively persuasive, attractive to the imagination rather than seeming merely to provide idle repetition, an empty cascade of superfluous reduplication. There is however no indication at all that there is a technical precision to the progress of effective praying, as if we should always proceed through the same orderly sequence. The repetition is poetic rather than literal, for the Father alone is the one to whom any of these requests are made.

Jeremias described this repetition as a beggar's logic. Just as the beggar's tireless repetition eventually pays off, Jesus is said to be encouraging a dogged persistence in prayer. In that case Jesus' meaning can only be that if a beggar can twist the arm of a reluctant passer-by, eventually relieving him of his loose change, how much more confident can we be of obtaining success when the object of our prayers is our heavenly Father.

The dominant emphasis of Jesus' words is not to explain

how to employ the correct sequence of petitions, nor merely to encourage a beggarly persistence, but rather to establish an environment of faithful expectancy for the prayers of his disciples. The two sentences almost precisely duplicate one another, word for word (7:7, 8). A similar stylistic device is common in Hebrew poetry. Very often in the Psalms we find verses in which the first and second lines are paired as duplicate statements. The rhyme is located in the meaning (not the sound of the words, as in traditional western European poetry) in what has been termed synonymous parallelism.

Jesus' teaching on prayer brings a new, extravagant multiplication to the existing poetic convention of simple parallelism. He employs not one but three paired statements. Twice Jesus connects asking with receiving, twice seeking and finding, twice knocking and opening. Jesus therefore combines parallelism with the 'rule of three' (that is, the familiar rhetorical device from folk tales and other oral traditions which is frequently used in Jesus' parables). What's more, not only do the two main sentences share an identical meaning, reinforced through the same sequence of three clauses, but the three pairs of clauses all make the same point, for there is ultimately no discernible difference between asking, seeking and knocking. This means that Jesus is making the same point with no less than a sixfold repetition, reinforcing his message to the greatest possible degree.

The method Jesus has frequently employed in his ethical teaching he now applies to the disciples' relationship with the Father. These verses are Jesus' messianic intensification of the power of prayer. The point of Jesus' extravagantly emphatic repetition is not so much to promote persistence as to provide confidence. The coming of the kingdom ushers in a new confidence that prayer really works.

Jesus' reassurance about prayer is further reinforced by his next parable, which explores prayer in terms of the father–child relationship. Once again a link can be made back to the Lord's Prayer and particularly to the opening phrase which addresses God as Father in the distinctive manner of Jesus. Bread and fish were the staple food of those who lived around Lake Galilee. Even the details of the parable are locally applicable: a round loaf could conceivably be confused with a round stone, just as a local catfish (*Clarias lazera*) could be confused with a snake. These details do more than lend an initial plausibility to the parable. As ever Jesus brings the new spirituality of the kingdom of heaven into direct contact with the ordinariness of everyday living.

Once again Jesus employs the 'rule of three': two examples of behaviour that would not be expected from earthly fathers, leading to the climactic assertion of the response to our requests that we can reasonably expect from the Father in heaven. Following on from the teaching about asking and receiving, this is Jesus' third consecutive triplet, each making essentially the same point. God can be trusted to answer prayers in a reliable and generous manner. The third statement in the third triplet takes on a distinctively climactic emphasis. It comes as the grand finale to these nine parallel statements, and is presented as a 'how much more' (*a fortiori*) statement.

This parable does more than promise that God answers prayer. It emphasises the Father's absolute trustworthiness, which is more reliable than that of the best of earthly fathers. Jesus is therefore dealing with our natural fears when approaching the transcendent God, the Lord of the cosmos. In the resurrection appearances and angelic visitations of the New Testament, it seems customary for those being visited to be reassured that there is nothing to fear. In the same way, Jesus uses his comparison between earthly fathers and God's fatherliness to melt away any residual fears among his disciples, both in their approach to God and in their petitions. Jesus' 'how much more' is designed to give confidence to his followers that they are praying to none other than the supreme Father in heaven.

The parable is not just about confidence in prayer, but also about intimacy. By turning from the general promise about answered prayer to this evocative parable, Jesus is establishing a clear context for intercession. God does not provide some kind of impersonal mechanism for answering prayers, an automated response when a request is properly presented. What Jesus commends is requests in the context of a rounded relationship, not requests in isolation. Petitionary prayer is set in the context of security – there is no need to fear a booby-trapped answer to prayer – and that security is then set in the context of intimacy. In Jesus' new revelation of the kingdom of heaven we do not pray to a remote and entirely inaccessible God who is distant in transcendence. Our requests are made to Abba Father, with whom Jesus calls us to enter and cultivate a new richness of right relationship. Jesus therefore completes his ethical teaching by reaffirming the two love commands that sum up the Law: loving God with our whole being and loving our neighbour as ourselves.

Right with Jesus (Mt 7:13–23)

Jesus' Great Sermon has reached its natural climax. He has called his disciples to right relationship both with the Father and with one another. His ethical teaching is complete when he teaches his Golden Rule. By withholding this until after he has explored right relationship with the Father he indicates that our vertical and horizontal relationships interconnect. Just as he stated that the two Old Testament love commands sum up the Law and the Prophets, he now declares that his own Golden Rule, and indeed the complete ethical teaching of the Great Sermon, can be seen as both summing up and fulfilling the Law and the Prophets. But the Sermon is not yet complete. There is still one more dimension of relationship that needs to be made right in order for us to inhabit the kingdom of heaven and live as true disciples.

The metaphor of two ways was familiar among the Jews. Jesus plainly describes his own teaching as the narrow road that leads to life. It is restricted in two senses: it is demanding and it is rigorous. As a result it will always remain, according to Jesus, a way adopted only by the minority. The connection between this narrow way and the gift of life once again speaks to the present and the future. The way of Jesus not only leads to the life of heaven, but it also brings abundant life in the present. Jesus' approach to holiness is consistently life-affirming. Here is no shrivelled ascetic, avoiding as much contact with others as possible. Jesus' higher righteousness positively encourages life to the full. Companionship, pleasure and laughter all find their place in the lifestyle he shared on the road with his closest disciples.

The added twist is the small gate by which the narrow way is entered. Jesus gives no explanation. He merely indicates that there needs to be a definite entry upon the narrow way, the life of discipleship. In the light of his resurrection, for Matthew the gate certainly signifies nothing less than a faith response to Jesus himself. The gate must first be entered by saving faith, and then the narrow path must be walked. The vital first step is a faith response to Jesus, but this is only the beginning. There is no suggestion that anyone could be entitled to pass through the gate and then put their feet up. The narrow path demands costly obedience and service, not easy-believism. Our call to follow Jesus is continually renewed in a lifelong journey into discipleship.

The next section strengthens the emphasis upon right relationship with Jesus, for he warns about false prophets who will ravage the church. Two descriptions of the false prophets are held in tension. On the one hand, their outward appearance is as harmless as sheep, even though their inner character and motivation is that of a ravenous wolf, the enemy of the true shepherd's flock. On the other hand, Jesus uses the metaphor of a tree only bearing one kind of fruit. This appears to suggest that identifying a false prophet is simple, but the first metaphor indicates that the first impression, in the likeness of a sheep, may be very favourable. Taken together, these two metaphors acknowledge the reality of false prophets in the future life of the church and warn that first impressions need to be tested by the nature of the lasting fruit.

The church is therefore called neither to be gullibly indiscriminate, nor to be impulsively judgemental. We must strenuously avoid two extremes: an indiscriminate desire to be inclusive of every conceivable viewpoint, irrespective of whether there is any assent to the essential gospel; and the equal and opposite error of a quasi-McCarthyite exclusion of every slight variant upon our own interpretation of the gospel. At the one extreme is radical and universalistic liberalism that can no longer confess that Jesus is Lord. At the other is reactionary and indiscriminate fundamentalism that is sweepingly dismissive of all outside its narrow sect. Jesus' precisely modulated parables reject both extremes, calling us instead to a discrimination that is always informed not by judgementalism but by the generosity of grace and the clarity of gospel truth.

Jesus shifts focus from our discernment to his own. He describes such false prophets coming to the final judgement and making their appeal for mercy. Their case is twofold: they address Jesus as Lord and they claim that their salvation has been conclusively demonstrated by their achievements in prophecy, deliverance and miracles. Their wonder-working has even been accomplished in the orthodox manner; that is, in the name of Jesus.

In part, Jesus is continuing to warn the future church to be discriminate. Although some false teachers may simply try to be persuasive, others will claim that their status as wonder-workers automatically vindicates their theology: 'If you see supernatural power in my meetings that must prove that God has given unqualified support to my teaching.' Modern Western pragmatism is no less vulnerable than illiterate societies to such enticement, but it is a snare. With gracious discernment we are called to test the teaching and test the fruit.

Although the presenting theme of this section is false prophets, the underlying theme is right relationship with Jesus. The claim of the false prophets that they have served him as Lord is roundly dismissed, but at the same time Jesus accepts the offered title. The Greek word for Lord, *Kurios*, can simply mean 'sir'. However, it was also used in the Greek translation of the Hebrew Old Testament to signify Jahweh; that is, God himself. Jesus is therefore pointing the way towards the early Christian confession that caused them so much trouble in the days of Caesar worship. They could not declare 'Caesar is Lord!' because a contradictory confession – 'Jesus is Lord!' – was pivotal to their faith. This lordship is manifest in four distinct ways within this passage.

First, the charismatic ministries of the early believers in prophecy, deliverance and healings were accomplished 'in the name of Jesus'. His authority and power made such actions possible.

Second, Jesus presents himself as the one who presides at the final judgement. He will serve as God's judge in determining who will be refused entry to the kingdom of heaven.

Third, relationship with Jesus will prove the determinative factor at this judgement. Despite the false prophets' claim to have served him, Jesus rejects them because there has been no direct contact, no faith relationship. The phrase 'I never knew you' corresponds to the rabbis' mildest form of exclusion, so it could simply mean 'there's nothing more between us'. However, in this context, with an emphasis upon right relationship with Jesus, the implication is stronger. Jesus' decisions at the last judgement will not be based upon miraculous exploits, nor upon credal conformity, but rather upon whether he knows us; that is, whether we have made a personal faith response to him.

Fourth, a genuine faith response will be expressed in the lifestyle of discipleship – true love for Jesus demonstrated in willing obedience. When Jesus dismisses the hangers-on, whose claims to authentic faith seemed at first so plausible, he condemns them as 'evil-doers'. Literally this means 'doers of lawlessness', from the Greek *anomia* (Matthew is quoting from the Greek translation of Psalm 6:8). This clearly indicates that the false prophets of whom Jesus speaks were antinomians – the polar opposite of the Judaising legalists with whom Paul had to contend. The antinomian false prophets attempted to interpret the coming of Jesus and the doctrines of grace as the 'abolition' of the Law in all its forms (Mt 5:17).

In dealing with the problem of false prophets, the concluding section of the Great Sermon is designed to open up a much broader theme: what it means for anyone to be in right relationship with Jesus.

Right with Jesus' teaching (Mt 7:24–27)

As a child I was sent to a Sunday school where one song was the almost universal favourite: 'The wise man built his house upon the rock'. The announcement of this song was the moment we had all been waiting for. The time-honoured actions permitted officially sanctioned mayhem: the one time when we were positively encouraged to make as much noise as possible while falling to the floor, enacting the ultimate fate of the foolish man's house built on sand. The great trick was not only to fall to the ground creating the maximum number of decibels, but also deftly to catch your neighbour's chair so that it 'accidentally' accompanied your abrupt crash to the floor. Of course, we quite missed the point of Jesus' story. For us, the collapse of the foolish man's house was no longer a terrible warning, but rather a wonderful moment to look forward to with growing expectancy.

Many home owners have become more familiar than they would wish to be with the dire consequences of inadequate foundations. As global warming continues to make London clay dry out and shrink, entire streets have begun to suffer from subsidence. Once, when we were house hunting, Claire and I visited a house with an extension at the back which leaned out at a drunken angle from the walls of the main structure. The owner was a merchant seaman and when I remarked upon the unusually sloping walls, he assured me that he had never noticed the problem. Given that he spent most of his life in ships that would often be leaning over at severe angles on the high seas, we gave him the benefit of the doubt. But we didn't buy the house.

My parents-in-law discovered a similar problem after moving into their new home. A beautiful house in a tranquil village, it had only been built a few years. Unfortunately it seemed that the builders had never troubled to find out from the old villagers that the plot of land they had acquired for development was the location of the old village pond. When the foundations are insecure or out of true, cosmetic repairs are worthless. Without major reconstruction, the entire building is destined to fall. The only way to repair the damage was to dig under the house and reinforce the foundations. For several months the house was not their own, reduced to a building site until its footings were made deep and secure.

Although adults readily understand the problems of building on sand rather than solid rock, we still often miss the point of Jesus' parable. The familiar Christian interpretation relates the parable to conversion. A life built on what we can do for God is a life built on sand. In order to be right with God we need to put our trust in Jesus Christ, the rock of our salvation. I would not wish for one moment to deny the necessity of saving faith, but this is not strictly the meaning of this particular parable. In fact Jesus makes his own meaning unmistakable in a repeated phrase: 'Everyone who hears these words of mine and puts them into practice' (7:24); 'Everyone who hears these words of mine and does not put them into practice' (7:26).

The parable with which Jesus completes the Sermon on the Mount is not one of conversion but one of discipleship. Jesus' specific concern is that we embrace the onerous task of seeking to live out his teaching. It is not enough to give nominal assent to Jesus' wisdom or goodness. It is not enough to offer him worship Sunday by Sunday. Just as Matthew's Gospel ends with the Great Commission's call to discipleship, the Sermon on the Mount ends with a similar theme. Quite simply, the life of discipleship is a life of obedience. In the details and decisions of everyday living, no matter how apparently inconsequential or trivial, we are called to a continuing obedience, taking the risks of putting into practice the teaching we have received from Jesus.

Severe storms come against both houses, with torrential rain, surging floods and a beating wind. Some treat religion as a way of escaping from life's difficulties, as if the right kind of faith might provide immunity from all pressures, disappointments and suffering. Jesus never shrinks from the harsher realities of life. He offers no fantasy nirvana, no life of ease among the lotus eaters. Just as he took in his stride the ultimate agony of the cross, Jesus calls his disciples to put his teaching into practice – not in order to evade life's hardships, but as a means of facing and overcoming them. The only universal promise of this parable is that the storms of life, whatever particular form they may take, are sure to come upon us all.

Only the storm makes apparent the decisive contrast between the rock and the sand. In a time of ease, the apparent reliability and safety of one kind of building is indistinguishable from the other. Jesus clearly indicates that the trials of life, far from being merely wanton and destructive, vindicate the genuine faith of living discipleship. At the same time, the storms of life expose the superficiality of nominal faith. Anyone with experience of pastoral care will know that different people respond to similar circumstances in quite different ways. Two people may have been given the same diagnosis of inoperable cancer: one renounces Christian faith in a downward spiral of anger and despair; the other rises to new heights of dignity as they stare death squarely in the eye and prepare themselves for resurrection life in Christ.

Jesus' concluding parable therefore conveys several pressing and practical implications. First, our response to Jesus and his teaching is absolutely critical and decisive. Second, Jesus calls us not merely to be hearers, but doers of his words. Third, the time of the storm is the time when living faith comes into its own, enabling us to stand secure. Fourth, having begun in the way of saving faith it is possible that later in life we can still turn to building upon sand. Our drift onto the sand may have been obvious – a conscious, deliberate and decisive repudiation of the ways of Jesus. But it can equally have been imperceptible – a creeping assimilation of the ways of this world, a gradual accommodation to peer pressure and the normal, instinctive and habitual values and priorities of our society.

When we were planning an extension to our home we began looking carefully at the extensions on other houses. Some were superb additions to the original house, beautifully integrated and built to last. Others were dismal: crude boxes roughly cemented to the existing building. It was difficult to see how planning permission had ever been given or building regulations complied with. We saw terrible cracks in the brickwork, walls listing at drunken angles, inadequately supported porches enacting a slow surrender to the merciless law of gravity. The original house had been built upon solid foundations, but the extension might as well have been built upon the sand.

These woeful extensions provide a stark warning. This is not a parable that can only be applied to our lives once, in the manner of Jesus' instruction that we need to be born again (Jn 3:3). Whenever we fail to put Jesus' teaching into practice, we begin to drift away from the rock. In all the extreme demands of Jesus, whether about unforgiveness and hatred, lustful thoughts or love of money, pride or self-interest, our lives can develop the spiritual and moral equivalent of ramshackle extensions, precariously built upon sand.

Where there is a warning in the words of Jesus there is usually also an invitation. Throughout this life there is always an opportunity for a fresh start; for secure foundations to be built anew. The implication is clear: whether the sandcastles of selfish living have been accidental or deliberate, newly erected or long-established, now is the time to abandon them. It's time to make sure that we are building a consistent life of discipleship on the secure foundations of Jesus' teaching. It's time to move onto the rock.

When preaching on this passage I sometimes suggest a practical response as I encourage a congregation to examine themselves before the risen Christ. Some will know that at present they have a sand problem in a particular attitude, relationship or aspect of life. In a practical expression of their desire to move onto the rock, I invite them to write down on a piece of paper the area of their life where they have been building on sand and leave it by the platform at the end of the meeting. Afterwards I ensure that the pieces of paper are taken out and destroyed – they are no one else's business. This simple action is symbolic, expressing a genuine and practical desire to move onto the rock. Of course, such a response does not require a public meeting. Even as you read this chapter, Jesus' pertinent parable can provoke self-examination. Is there a particular area of your life where you have been building on the sand? And are you prepared, right now, to choose to move back onto the rock?

The response of the crowd

Matthew underlines this third dimension of right relationship with Jesus himself in his concluding description of the response of the crowd. They marvel at the content of his teaching, which is hardly surprising, for they have just witnessed the greatest sermon ever preached. More than that, they recognise Jesus to be a great teacher with an extraordinary authority, incomparably superior to the ordinary Jewish teachers of the Law. The astonishment of the crowd provokes an inevitable question: Who is this man?

Their focus upon Jesus himself grows naturally from his teaching. His life and message were a perfect match, with no hint of self-contradiction. What he taught he embodied. From his claims to provide a definitive interpretation of scripture – 'but I say' – he set himself above the rabbis and even Moses. From his claims to fulfil the Law and usher in the kingdom, he presented himself not simply as the messenger, but integral, indeed central, to his message. He describes himself as the definitive Teacher, the final Judge, and the one rightly addressed as Lord. When Jesus questioned his disciples at Caesarea Philippi concerning opinions about him, he was not indulging idle curiosity. This gentle initial canvassing of public opinion led to Jesus' most searching question: 'But what about you? Who do *you* say I am?' (Mt 16:15). The same direct and provocative question is implicit throughout Jesus' ministry for everyone who hears him or speaks with him. There is no adequate response to his extraordinary message without a response to Jesus himself.

The Sermon on the Mount is so much more than a mere collection of ethical teaching. Jesus invites his hearers not just to attempt to adopt his code of conduct, but to make a faith response to the Teacher. The only way to enter the new life of the kingdom, and to enjoy right relationship both with the Father and with our brothers and sisters, is first to enter right relationship with Jesus Christ. This is true in conversion and remains true in daily living. If our relationship with Jesus is marginalised, right relationships with the Father and fellow believers are bound to deteriorate.

The manifesto of discipleship is nothing less than a call to conversion. Only by faith in Jesus can we enter the narrow gate and discover the new way of living to which he has called us: *the way of fulfilment* in the inverted priorities of the Beatitudes; *the way of perfection* in pursuit of the higher righteousness; *the way of liberation*, freed from the petty constraints of human religion and the tyranny of materialism; and *the way of right relationships*, with our Father in heaven, with brothers and sisters in the community of disciples and, above all, with Jesus himself, our Teacher and Master, Saviour and Lord.

The responsibility of the church is immense. By our words and actions we can establish or destroy the credibility of Jesus Christ in the eyes of the world. At the dawn of the third Christian millennium we need something more fundamental than new strategies, new structures, new songs or new marketing methods. The church needs to be reborn in response to Jesus' call to discipleship. If we are willing to embrace once again the adventure of uncompromised discipleship, the Sermon on the Mount still has the power to bring about a re-invigoration, a re-awakening of the church. If the new millennium is going to see a return of the Western world to the Christian faith, the followers of Christ will need to look a lot more like their Master. We need nothing less than a recovery of whole-life discipleship in imitation of Jesus Christ, a life built upon the rock of purity of heart and self-giving love. We need to discover once again the courage of living faith that offers no excuses, pleads no special allowances, requests no postponement, but willingly and urgently responds to the invitation of Jesus: 'Come, follow me.'

Selected Bibliography

Classic preachers' commentaries

Augustine, *Our Lord's Sermon on the Mount*
J. Calvin, *Commentary on a Harmony of the Evangelists, Matthew, Mark and Luke*
J. Chrysostom, *Homilies on St Matthew's Gospel*
D. Dickson, *Matthew*
M. Luther, *The Sermon on the Mount*
J. C. Ryle, *Expository Thoughts on the Gospels*
C. H. Spurgeon, *The Gospel of the Kingdom*
J. Wesley, *Sermons on the Sermon on the Mount*

Modern commentaries and critical studies

G. R. Beasley-Murray, *Jesus and the Kingdom of God* (Exeter: Paternoster, 1986).
S. Blanch, *The Way of Blessedness* (London: Hodder & Stoughton, 1985).
D. Bonhoeffer, *The Cost of Discipleship* (English translation, London: SCM, 1959).
P. Bonnard, *L'Evangile selon Saint Matthieu*, 2nd edition (Neuchatel: Delachaux et Niestle, 1970).
G. Bornkamm, *Jesus of Nazareth* (English translation, London: Hodder & Stoughton, 1960).
D. Carson, *The Sermon on the Mount* (Grand Rapids: Baker, 1978).

D. Carson, *Matthew (Expositor's Bible Commentary)* (Grand Rapids: Zondervan, 1984).

D. Daube, *The New Testament and Rabbinic Judaism* (London: Athlone, 1956).

W. D. Davies, *The Setting of the Sermon on the Mount* (Cambridge: CUP, 1964).

J. Drury, *The Parables in the Gospels* (London: SPCK, 1985).

J. D. Dunn, *Christology in the Making* (London: SCM, 1980).

J. C. Fenton, *Saint Matthew (Pelican Gospel Commentaries)* (London: Penguin, 1963).

R. T. France, *Matthew: Evangelist and Teacher* (Exeter: Paternoster, 1989).

R. T. France, *Matthew (Tyndale series)* (Leicester: IVP, 1985).

R. Guelich, *The Sermon on the Mount: a foundation for understanding* (Waco: Word, 1982).

R. Gundry, *Matthew: a commentary on his literary and theological art* (Grand Rapids: Eerdmans, 1982).

A. M. Hunter, *Design for Life: an exposition of the Sermon on the Mount* (London: SCM, 1953, 1965).

D. Hill, *The Gospel of Matthew (New Century Bible Series)* (London: Marshall, Morgan & Scott, 1972).

J. Jeremias, *New Testament Theology* (English translation, London: SCM, 1971).

J. Jeremias, *The Parables of Jesus* (English translation, London: SCM, 1963).

J. Jeremias, *The Prayers of Jesus* (English translation, London: SCM, 1958).

F. Kermode, *The Genesis of Secrecy* (London: Harvard University Press, 1979).

J. Kingsbury, *Matthew: Structure, Christology, Kingdom* (Philadelphia: Fortress Press, 1975).

W. Kummel, *Theology of the New Testament* (English translation, London: SCM, 1974).

G. Ladd, *The Presence of the Future* (Grand Rapids: Eerdmans, 1974).

D. M. Lloyd-Jones, *Studies in the Sermon on the Mount* (Leicester: IVP, 1976).

T. W. Manson, *The Sayings of Jesus* (London: SCM, 1949).

B. F. Meyer, *The Aims of Jesus* (London: SCM, 1979).

P. S. Minear, *Matthew: The Teacher's Gospel* (London: DLT, 1984).

N. Perrin, *Jesus and the Language of the Kingdom* (London: SCM, 1976).

R. Schnackenburg, *The Moral Teaching of the New Testament* (English translation, Tunbridge Wells: Burns & Oates, 1965).

E. Schweizer, *The Good News According to Matthew* (English translation, London: SPCK, 1976).

G. Stanton (ed.), *The Interpretation of Matthew* (London: SPCK, 1983).

G. Stanton, *A Gospel for a New People: Studies in Matthew* (Edinburgh: T. & T. Clark, 1991).

J. Stott, *Christian Counter Culture – The Sermon on the Mount* (Leicester: IVP, 1978). Second edition: *The Message of the Sermon on the Mount* (Leicester: IVP, 1992).

R. Tasker, *The Gospel According to Saint Matthew* (London: Tyndale (IVP), 1961).

W. B. Tatum, *In Quest of Jesus* (London: SCM, 1983).

H. Thielicke, *Life Can Begin Again: Sermons on the Sermon on the Mount* (English translation, Philadelphia: Fortress Press, 1963).

G. Vermes, *Jesus the Jew* (London: Collins, 1973).

The Anabaptist tradition asks searching questions, even when those in other traditions are ultimately unable to accept an approach that requires an absolute separation between church and state, and an unreserved commitment to pacifism. Much of the distinctive approach of the radical reformers is grounded in their interpretation and application of the Sermon on the Mount. The following bibliography identifies some of the key texts either from within or much influenced by Anabaptists.

W. Klaassen (ed.), *Anabaptism in Outline* (Scottdale: Herald, 1981).

D. Kraybill, *The Upside Down Kingdom* (Scottdale: Herald, 1978).

A. Kreider, *Journey Towards Holiness* (Basingstoke: Marshall, Morgan & Scott, 1986).

J. Lasserre, *War and the Gospel* (English translation, London: James Clarke, 1962).

R. Sider, *Christ and Violence* (Scottdale: Herald, 1979).

R. Sider, *Rich Christians in an Age of Hunger*, 2nd edition (London: Hodder & Stoughton, 1990).

L. Verduin, *The Anatomy of a Hybrid* (Grand Rapids: Eerdmans, 1976).

J. Wallis, *Agenda for Biblical People* (New York: Harper & Row, 1976).

J. Wallis, *The Call to Conversion* (Tring: Lion, 1981).

J. Yoder (ed.), *God's Revolution: The Witness of Eberhard Arnold*

J. Yoder, *The Politics of Jesus* (Grand Rapids: Eerdmans, 1972).

Two classic studies of different Christian models of the relationship between church, state and culture provide an invaluable framework when considering the societal implications of the ethics of the Sermon on the Mount:

C. H. Kraft, *Christianity in Culture* (New York: Orbis, 1979).

H. R. Niebuhr, *Christ and Culture* (New York: Harper & Row, 1951; New York: Paulist Press, 1984).